DECORATIVE ORNAMENT
VOL. 3

DECORATIVE ORNAMENT

ARRANGED AND EDITED BY WOLFGANG HAGENEY

BELVEDERE

EDITION BELVEDERE CO. LTD., ROME - MILAN (ITALY)

BELVEDERE
DESIGNBOOK
FASHION
TEXTILES
GRAPHIC
DESIGNS
VOLUME 17
PART III

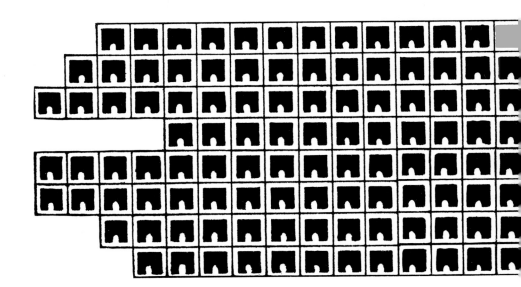

DECORATIVE ORNAMENT

PUBLISHED BY
EDITION BELVEDERE CO. LTD.
ROME-MILAN (ITALY)

© COPYRIGHT 1984
BY EDITION BELVEDERE SRL

PRINTED IN ITALY BY
STUDIO TIPOGRAFICO, ROME
PHOTOLITHOGRAPHY BY
BELVEDERE LABORATORIES, ROME
COLOR SEPARATIONS BY
ART COLOR OFFSET, ROME
LAYOUT, GRAPHIC DESIGN
& TYPE SETTING BY
STUDIO BELVEDERE, ROME
ART DIRECTOR: HWH & BVR

PRINT PRODUCTION: MARCELLO CARMELLINI
STUDIO PRODUCTION: ROSA LENGSFELD
EDITOR & PUBLISHER: WOLFGANG H. HAGENEY

EDITION BELVEDERE CO. LTD.
00196 ROME/ITALY, PIAZZALE FLAMINIO, 19
TEL. (06) 360.44.88/360.29.60

ISBN 88-7070-031-3

ORNAMENT

The time was the turn of the century: still shortly before the conclusive triumph of machine and technology, on the eve of the total Industrial Revolution with its inexorable drive towards mechanization and rationalization, its flood of mass-produced goods, its irresistable depersonalization of individual forms of expression and creation: it was at this time that for a brief moment, in Europe, art (and most of all, the handcrafts and the decorative arts) sought to oppose that all-devouring Moloch, the new Zeitgeist.

But since technological and material development was not to be halted, an attempt was made to exploit at least the possibilities of the conflict so as to obtain, through Art, a symbiosis which would bring the worlds of "Technique/Function/Reason" and "Man/Psyche/Nature" in harmony with each other.

What was hoped for was the possibility of creating a counterbalance. Man would not be simply the function and the target of production methods and their mathematical conformity; rather, he would realize himself in private things, in the canon of forms of associative thoughts and feelings, in accord with himself, with Nature, and with the reality around him.

What counted was to propose an alternative that would offer the chance of self-realization through "another way of living": the "I" determined not by the pressures of mechanical and functional conceptions of purpose, but rather legitimized out of its most innate needs: sensitivity to color, the language of forms, the awareness of style, or the play of emotions.

The growing knowledge of the psyche, the meaning of dreams, the development of psychoanalysis, the discoveries of graphology, the first dawning of women's emancipation: in a time of upheaval as well as dehumanization, alienation and mass production, these were the pillars which could support a program for a new religion, a new morality, a new artistic sensibility - a new cult, even: Art Nouveau, the art of the psychic life, the oneness of Life and Art.

A quest to re-shape and re-create the totality of Man's experience of life not simply anew, but also from within, from the center outwards, to pierce through. The new perceptions of psychoanalysis were not to be denied in Art Nouveau. More and more, artists frequented greenhouses and conservatories to submit themselves to detailed studies of the exotically floral, the profusively exuberant, the ambiguously entwining. And they belived they could fix forever, in the noble and tender shoots and plants, in fern and foliage, the center and origin of all that profusion which the society of the time looked on with so much uneasiness: the sphere of influence of psychology.

It was becoming unmistakably clearer that behind external forms of appearance and their world of symbol there lurks a second reality that evades the grasp of reason and that exerts more influence on Man's behavior than he is accustomed to believe.

And so, in the greenhouses of an inner world, during the last summer nights of a dying age, artists worked to transform the extravagant growth of human psychic life into ornament, to beautify visually the roots and flowers of dream and reality, while at the same time emancipated Woman did not shy from the light of day, but sought in the applied arts to experience with utter commitment and an almost religious passion the dissolution of her prescribed roles - sought, in the ornament of Art Nouveau, a new religious creed.

And this explained the enormous diffusion of the art magazines springing up everywhere, publications that had the quality of fine books and which were more than sample catalogs reflecting the creative formulations of the feeling of the time: indeed they were to be treated and interpreted as the catechism of the new religion being just then proclaimed.

And what was being proclaimed was the unity of experience, the total work of art, the formulation of a complete lifestyle. The longing for a lost originality was made manifest, a longing for the atmosphere, the marvels of the worlds of fairytale and romance.

What was sought was a consummate, all-consuming beauty, harmony and grace of movement and, ultimately, a sustaining order in accordance with Nature to serve as a foundation for the totality of the life and feeling of Man.

The aesthetic of Art Nouveau placed the green world directly in the center of its theory of ornament, but alongside that it permitted abstract forms too, though generally only those with a plant-like movement, or line ornaments whose play of motion was based on long, thin stems or uninterruptedly ondulating line. The newly-discovered depths of the psyche, different planes of reality superimposed, the free association of dream elements, the use of an almost filtered palette of natural colors (corresponding to the intermediates tones of Nature as experienced in dreams), and the bursting out of habitual formal dimensions - all these allowed the birth of a new feeling, a new ornamentation, a kind of imprint that, despite it surfaceness and lack of shadow, despite its poster-like effect, was to resemble an impression of the psyche.

The artists of Art Nouveau must have had a sense that they were preparing the scene for the final celebration of an era that was approaching its death. It would be a festival whose dance floor rested on pillars of luxurious blossoms and so was not immune to the passage of time, but was in fact stirred by the breath and the music of an early death.

Consequently what was to be done was prepare the stage, sensually and erotically, manically and passionately, for an elegant Dance of Death, seeing that already the functionaries of the new industrial age stood ready at every ballroom exit with their execution orders in hand.

The sublimest, the most symbolically pregnant flora - the formal, but also spiritual, essence of Art Nouveau, that could be promised, certainly, the shortest but most abundant of lives - would be artistically and meaningfully arranged so that their pallid and mannered beauty could be felt and admired for one last time.

What was wanted was to move towards death in formal dress: to present Death not with a limp body but rather with one that was richly turned out and trim.

Was not everything after all only a feverish illusion? Or was there not born overnight a desire that sought to place itself against the rays of the early morning sun in a drop of dew?

In this spiritual climate and in this social context it was easy to overcome much that was traditional, to unite ornamentally the archaic and the classical, the flowing and the stift, the West alongside the Far East. Here, ornamentation no longer had only the function of decorating, complementing, accenting or even of remaining neutral. Now it must sprout, grow, proliferate, burst out, develop its own set of laws, become the all-dominating focus of the scene. Ornament: not only as formal element, but rather an independent and sovereign embodiment of the content itself, with a dramatic inclination towards arrogance.

In an awareness of the coming end of things, hierarchical problems - the relation between space and time, of space and surface, or of form and color - played only a subordinate role.

In the attempt to use Art Nouveau to infiltrate the established aesthetic order, to infuse a new consciousness, such problems had only incidental significance.

In place of "Form" there was now "Deformation", or the use of different pictorial and reality levels in complete disregard of the circumstances actually present in the foreground: ornament, therefore, as the catalyst of art and psychology, of art and life, as a synthesis of desire and reality.

The consciousness of "bloom and perish", appropriate to the botanical nature of Art Nouveau, permitted liberties hitherto unknown in art. The implacable approach of the new, proliferating industrial society quickened the pace. And so the final act began (at the end, already a search for time past), the curtain rung up with the dying away of a cultural episode.

What was the fascination, the mystery, the aura, the erotic and narcotic in the epoch of Art Nouveau? A style which in its few years in the garden of Western art squandered, like the fragrance of flowers in bloom in the tropical night, all its élan, its unbounded fantasy, and its inexhaustible richness of form. A blossoming - infatuating as the perfume of orchids, with the ornamental simplicity and power of the lily - a new style: Art Nouveau, Jugendstil, stile floreale.

Two scenes from literature come to mind: the dance of the maidens from "Les filles du feu" of Gérard de Nerval, and the last ball in the house of the Guermantes from Marcel Proust's "A la recherche du temps perdu". As one depicts an early root of Art Nouveau, so the other shows it in its decline. One scene presents living ornament, a picture of youthfulness and the fragrance of flowers. Opening themselves like the calyxes of flowers, the young girls dance to the rhythm of the old traditional songs of the Valois. On a grassy surface surrounding a stately tree, the dance of maidens forms, as it moves, patterns that are continually new. Dappled with moonlight, the dancing figures and the fairy-tale surroundings create an ornament that is enhanced by the delicate grace of the girls bodies themselves.

Alongside this image from the early days of ornamental creativity as sketched by Gérard de Nerval (Les filles du feu, Sylvie) can be placed one from the time when Art Nouveau is drawing to a close, a portrait of the transience of all flowers, crystallized in a cube-like sample of premature old age.

The spontaneous memories of Marcel Proust (A la recherche du temps perdu, Le temps retrouvé), memories of a time of refined sensibility and subtle nuance, contrast the shadows of the bygone embellishments of the Guermantes salon, bring them together in a spectral masquerade, marshalled into a sprightly dance of death. A scene of elegantly garbed skeletons, come together for the last ball before the grey dawn of imminent industrialization.

Blooming and withering compose themselves into the rhythm of a dance, a dance like that demonstrated by the American choreographer Loie Fuller in her "Serpentine Dances", into the abstracting form of ornament that flows yet persists, that turns in upon itself, interweaving all of life.

Overflowing growth, the asymmetry of the green world, intensification into an aestheticization of life and art which knows itself through the senses, into an aesthetic of life stylized into transience, a form of expression that lays claim to being more than simply a new style of decadence.

Art Nouveau opens with an unbounded impulse towards decorative form. In the sensitively undulating line, Art Nouveau found all the charms of abstractness and runic originality, and it immediately chose it as a new and independent means of expression. It took for its purposes the language of plant forms, and in combinations of exotic plants like the lady's-slipper and the iris together with symbols of the female, it generates an erotic tension which, graphically, conveys the effect of a diffusion through space, or that favors creation of precious and transparent objects such as glasses and vases overlaid with flowing ornament, and gives them speech like Emile Gallé's "verres parlants". The strikingly-named "stile floreale" creates pieces of jewellery of entrancing tenderness, it hangs lamps of blooming and airy lightness over the entrances of the Paris Metro: an enduring emblem of Art Nouveau.

Another European variant of the Jugendstil follows the rhythmic line of Nature, weaves flowing forms like growths of seaweed into an invisible, submarine kingdom, exempts objects from their thing-ness. Organic ornament grows into magic sign.

And ornament does not serve as external decoration: it is a structural element, it transforms the world of everyday into ever freer rhythms. Ornament becomes a bearer of function: it changes a doorknob into a gesture, it receives the guest at the first stairway with welcoming gestures and leads him imperceptably into an inner space with high, bright glass domes, where generously matched fabrics and carpets with delicate patterns suggest a new sense of living.

The vegetative origin of the ornaments, surcharged with a kind of fragile tenderness, gives off a trace of the breath of floral growth. They awake sensory perception, stir the sense of touch, evoke fragrances, diffuse an opaque light.

The refined enhancement of forms is complemented by a delicately shaded coloring which, pale and toned down, calls for the intermediate tones of translucent lamps.

The aestheticizing of life hints broadly at a world of the aesthetic of transience, at a nostalgic dream world where the frontiers between dream and reality dissolve into pure ornament that - here abstract, there showing the cup of a flower growing out of the charming body of a youth or maiden - desires to lead onwards from dream into dream. The new, bio-"logic" forms point to a pre-rational, vegetal existence. A sense of transience clings to their shapes. Shapes, these, that occur in an unfamiliar, iridescent light, and that flow into the utopia of an Art--life, where, overpoweringly beautiful and transient, the magical fragrance of exotic plants streams forth.

XIII

Negli anni attorno alla fine del secolo scorso, poco prima del definitivo avvento delle macchine e della tecnica, alla vigilia della rivoluzione industriale totale con la sua inesorabile spinta alla meccanizzazione e alla razionalizzazione, l'immissione sul mercato di prodotti di massa e l'inarrestabile processo di massificazione di tutte le forme di espressione e di creazione individuali, l'arte in Europa (e in particolare l'artigianato e le arti decorative) tentò di opporsi per un breve arco di tempo a questo nuovo spirito dell'epoca, a questo Moloch divoratore.

Ma dal momento che lo sviluppo tecnico e materiale non si poteva arrestare, si cercò almeno di sfruttare le possibilità del conflitto per arrivare attraverso l'arte ad una simbiosi, che conciliasse il mondo della "tecnica-funzione-razionalità" con quello dell' "uomo-anima-natura".

Si sperava di creare una compensazione sulla base della coesistenza: l'uomo non soltanto come puro obiettivo e scopo dei metodi di produzione e delle loro matematiche leggi interne, ma autorealizzato nel privato, nel canone formale del pensiero associativo e della sensibilità, in armonia con se stesso e con il mondo oggettivo circostante. Si trattava, appunto, di offrire un'alternativa che fosse valida anche per la realizzazione di un "altro modo di vita": l' "Io" non determinato dall'obbligo di idee meccaniche e funzionali, ma legittimato dai bisogni individuali come il senso del colore, il linguaggio delle forme, la consapevolezza dello stile, la sfera emozionale.

L'affiorare dell'inconscio, l'interpretazione dei sogni, lo sviluppo della psicanalisi, le scoperte della grafologia, così come i primi segnali e il primo avvio dell'emancipazione femminile: in un'epoca di svolta verso la massificazione, la produzione in serie e l'alienazione, queste erano le colonne sulle quali si poteva costruire una nuova religione, una nuova morale, una nuova sensibilità artistica, addirittura un nuovo culto, lo stile floreale, l'arte della vita interiore, l'unione di arte e vita. Il tentativo non solo di ristrutturare tutte le sfere vitali dell'essere umano, ma di intervenire dal di dentro, partendo dal centro.

Le nuove conoscenze acquisite con la psicanalisi lasciarono tracce evidenti nell'arte dello "Jugendstil". Un numero sempre maggiore di artisti affollava le serre per sottoporre a studi attenti forme vegetali bizzarre, piante lussureggianti, rampicanti esotici. Si credeva, appunto, di poter cogliere nelle forme vegetali e nelle piante più rare e delicate, nelle felci e nel fogliame il germe e il nucleo primario di tutte quelle deformazioni alle quali la società di allora guardava con sempre maggior disagio: la sfera di influenza della psicologia. Si intuiva sempre più chiaramente come dietro le forme esteriori e il loro mondo simbolico fosse in agguato una seconda realtà, non percepibile razionalmente, che poteva influire sul comportamento dell'uomo più di quanto era portato a credere.

Fu così che, nelle ultime notti estive di un'epoca che stava volgendo al tramonto, gli artisti esplorarono le serre di un mondo interiore per dare forma ornamentale agli istinti esplosi come polloni nella vita psichica dell'uomo, per abbellire visivamente le radici e i fiori del sogno e della realtà, mentre la donna emancipata non temeva la luce del giorno per sperimentare nelle arti decorative con estremo impegno e con un fervore religioso la liberazione da un ruolo prestabilito, per cercare nello "Jugendstil" addirittura una nuova professione di fede. Ciò spiega anche l'enorme diffusione delle riviste artistiche sorte un po' dovunque (non di rado a carattere bibliofilo), che non solo rispecchiavano, come una sorta di campionari del nuovo stile le idee e le forme del tempo, ma addirittura venivano trattate e interpretate come il catechismo della religione appena annunciata.

Fu proclamata l'unità dell'esperienza, l'opera d'arte totale, la formazione di uno stile di vita complessivo. Divenne manifesta la nostalgia della primitività perduta, del tono incantato e del meraviglioso, presenti nel mondo delle favole e delle leggende. Si andava alla ricerca della bellezza totale e struggente, dell'armonia e della grazia dei movimenti e, infine, di un ordine ultimo, determinato dalla natura, che potesse servire come base per la vita fisica e psichica dell'uomo.

L'arte dello "Jugendstil" mise al centro della sua ricerca ornamentale tutto il mondo vegetale, lasciando comunque spazio anche alle forme astratte, per lo più con ghirigori vegetali o con ornamenti lineari, il cui movimento era giocato su lunghi, esili steli o su tratti fortemente arcuati.

Le profondità della psiche scoperte di recente, le stratificazioni di diversi livelli di realtà, il libero accostamento di elementi onirici, il diffuso impiego di una tavolozza di colori naturali (corrispondente alle tonalità della natura vissuta nel sogno), come pure l'uscita dalle dimensioni formali tradizionali, diedero vita a un nuovo sentimento, a una nuova forma di ornamento, a una sorta di marchio che, nonostante la sua unidimensionalità e l'assenza di chiaroscuri e nonostante l'effetto cartellonistico, doveva assomigliare a un'impronta dell'anima.

Gli artisti dello "Jugendstil" dovevano avere intuito che si accingevano ad allestire l'ultima festa di un'epoca destinata a scomparire. Una festa, la cui pista da ballo ondeggiava sui pilastri formati dai calici di rampicanti e che dunque, proprio per questa ragione, non era protetta contro la caducità, anzi era già avvolta dall'alito e dal canto di una morte precoce. Di conseguenza si doveva mettere in scena, sensualmente ed eroticamente, maniacalmente e appassionatamente una elegiaca danza macabra, dal momento che gli interpreti dell'avvento industriale già premevano alle porte delle sale con i loro mandati esecutivi.

La flora più sublime e più carica di simboli - essenza formale ed al tempo stesso spirituale dello "Jugendstil", che senza dubbio poteva promettere una vita estremamente breve ma esuberante - fu drappeggiata in modo artistico e significativo, dal momento che si voleva sentire e ammirare per l'ultima volta la sua bellezza esangue e raffinata. Si voleva godere fino in fondo il lento estinguersi, offrendo alla morte non un corpo esaurito, ma riccamente addobbato. Tutto questo non era forse una stanca, vaneggiante illusione? Oppure era la volontà, nata durante la notte, che all'alba nelle gocce della rugiada tentava di contrapporsi ai raggi del sole?

In questo clima spirituale e in questo ambito sociale era facile superare molte barriere tradizionali e unire nell'elemento ornamentale l'arcaico al classico, il fluttuante all'immobile, il mondo dell'Occidente a quello dell'Estremo Oriente. Qui l'ornamento non doveva più limitarsi ad abbellire, articolare, sottolineare o ad avere una funzione neutrale. Ora poteva sbocciare, avviticchiarsi, lussureggiare, germogliare, sviluppare una propria legge interna, diventare centro focale della scena. L'ornamento non solo come elemento formale, ma come incarnazione autonoma e assoluta del contenuto stesso, con una disposizione giocosa all'arroganza. - In considerazione della fine imminente, problemi gerarchici come la relazione di spazio e tempo, spazio e superficie o forma e colore non potevano che avere un ruolo subordinato. Nel tentativo di infiltrarsi attraverso lo "Jugendstil" nell'ordine estetico prestabilito facendovi penetrare una nuova coscienza, quei problemi rivestivano un'importanza marginale. Al posto della "forma" ora era in primo piano la "deformazione" o l'uso di piani diversi della realtà e dell'immagine senza tener conto del dato reale: l'ornamento come catalizzatore di arte e psicologia, di arte e vita, come sintesi di desiderio e realtà.

La cognizione del "fiorire e appassire", conforme al carattere vegetale dello "Jugendstil", consentì nell'arte libertà mai prima conosciute. Il costante avanzamento della nuova società industriale in espansione creava una situazione di urgenza. E così ebbe inizio quest'atto conclusivo (in ultima analisi già una ricerca dell'età perduta), che già preannunciava la fine di una stagione culturale.

Quali sono stati il fascino, il mistero, il fluido, l'elemento erotico e narcotizzante dell'epoca dello "Jugendstil"? Uno stile che, come il profumo di fiori sbocciati in una notte tropicale, ha bruciato nell'arco di pochi anni il suo slancio, la sua immensa fantasia e l'inesauribile ricchezza delle sue forme nel giardino dell'arte occidentale. Una fioritura - stordente come il profumo dell'orchidea, severa nell'ornamento del giglio - un nuovo stile: art nouveau/modern style/stile floreale.

Dal repertorio letterario si stagliano due scene: la danza delle fanciulle nelle "Filles du feu" di Gérard de Nerval e l'ultima festa in casa dei Guermantes in "A la recherche du temps perdu" di Marcel Proust. Esse rappresentano l'una una radice lontana, l'altra lo sfiorire dello "Jugendstil".

La prima scena disegna un ornamento vivo, un'immagine di giovinezza e di essenze floreali. Aprendosi come calici di fiori le fanciulle danzano al ritmo di antiche chansons dei Valois. Il cerchio delle fanciulle crea sul tappeto erboso circondato da alberi ad alto fusto un disegno che si trasforma continuamente. Le figure danzanti illuminate dal chiarore lunare e lo scenario fiabesco circostante danno origine a un ornamento, che viene potenziato dalla grazia raffinata delle fanciulle.

Accanto a questa immagine schizzata da Gérard de Nerval ("Le filles du feu", "Sylvie"), che risale alla preistoria delle forme ornamentali, si può collocare - cronologicamente già verso la fine dello "Jugendstil" - un quadro della caducità di tutto il fiorire, cristallizzato nel motivo della vecchiaia precoce. Allo spontaneo riandare con la memoria di Marcel Proust ("A la recherche du temps perdu", "Le temps retrouvé") ai tempi delle più delicate raffinatezze e delle allusioni sfumate si contrappongono le ombre degli splendori passati dei saloni dei Guermantes, raccolte in una mascherata spettrale e disposte in una danza macabra. Una scena di scheletri finemente addobbati, raccolti una notte per l'ultimo ballo prima dell'alba della nuova età industriale.

Fioritura e sfioritura si saldano dunque nel ritmo di una danza, come quella inventata dall'americana Loie Fuller nelle sue "Danze serpentine", nella forma astrattizzante dell'ornamento che scorre, si blocca, ruota su se stesso, penetra l'intero tessuto vitale. Crescita traboccante, asimmetria vegetale, potenziamento in una estetizzazione di arte e vita, che si sa sensuale e si stilizza in una estetica della vita nell'effimero, una forma espressiva che vuole essere altro e più che non soltanto un nuovo stile della decadenza. Lo "Jugendstil" esplode con una irrefrenabile intenzione formale in direzione dell'ornamento. Nella linea sensuale e flessuosa trova quel fascino dell'astrattezza e dell'origine runica, che l'"art nouveau" sceglie subito come nuovo, autonomo strumento di espressione.

Lo "Jugendstil" si serve del linguaggio formale vegetale e innesca attraverso l'interrelazione di piante esotiche come il cipripedio e l'iris con simboli femminili una tensione erotica, che graficamente sembra sfondare lo spazio, impreziosisce e rende trasparenti gli oggetti, riveste vasi e coppe di ornamenti floreali e li fa parlare, come i "verres parlants" di Emile Gallé.

Quello che giustamente è stato definito "stile floreale" produce gioielli di incantevole finezza, appende sugli ingressi del Métro di Parigi lampade impalpabili e senza peso come calici di fiori. Un segno duraturo dell'"art nouveau". - Un'altra variante europea dell'"art nouveau" segue la linea ritmica della natura, fa fluttuare in un regno sottomarino invisibile forme ondeggianti come vegetazioni di alghe, libera gli oggetti della loro oggettualità. L'ornamento organico si avviticchia in un segno magico.

L'ornamento non serve alla decorazione esterna, è elemento strutturale, trasforma il mondo della quotidianità in ritmi sempre più liberi. L'ornamento diventa portatore di una funzione: trasforma la maniglia in un atto, accoglie l'ospite sul primo scalino della casa con gesto di invito e lo conduce, quasi impercettibile, negli ambienti interni con alte, luminose cupole di vetro, dove stoffe stese a profusione e tappezzerie dai disegni delicati suggeriscono un nuovo senso della vita.

L'origine vegetale degli ornamenti, sovraccarichi di segni di una estrema delicatezza, fa avvertire il soffio profumato della fioritura. Destano sensazioni sensuali, sfiorano il senso del gusto, evocano fragranze, diffondono luce opaca. Al raffinato potenziamento delle forme corrisponde una ricerca del colore costantemente sfumato, armonizzato e sbiadito, che cerca le tonalità intermedie della luminosità traslucida.

L'estetizzazione dell'esistenza invita a un mondo dell'estetica dell'effimero, a un mondo onirico senza turbamenti, dove i confini tra sogno e realtà si dissolvono nel puro ornamento, che - ora in forme astratte, ora disegnando il calice di un fiore dal quale escono i corpi aggraziati di fanciulle e di efebi - conduce al sogno nel sogno. Le nuove forme bio-"logiche" rimandano a un'esistenza prerazionale, vegetale. Le figure in cui esse si realizzano sono cariche di un senso dell'effimero.

Figure che amano una luce dalle strane iridescenze e approdano all'utopia di una esistenza artistica, che, straordinariamente bella ed effimera, effonde il profumo magico di piante esotiche.

Es war zur Zeit der Jahrhundertwende, noch kurz vor dem endgültigen Aufbegehren von Maschine und Technik, am Vorabend der totalen industriellen Revolution mit ihrem unvermeidlichen Zwang zur Mechanisierung und Rationalisierung, mit ihrem Ausstoß an Massenprodukten und ihrer unaufhaltsamen Vermassung individueller Ausdrucks- und Gestaltungsformen, als sich in Europa die Kunst (und vor allem das Kunsthandwerk und das Kunstgewerbe) für eine kurze Zeitspanne dem neuen Zeitgeist, diesem allesfressenden Moloch, entgegenzustellen versuchte.

Da aber die technisch-materielle Entwicklung nicht aufzuhalten war, bemühte man sich, wenigstens die Möglichkeiten des Konflikts zu nutzen, um durch die Kunst zu einer Symbiose zu gelangen, die die Welt von "Technik/Funktion/Ratio" mit der von "Mensch/Seele/Natur" in Einklang bringen wollte.

Man hoffte, auf der Basis der Koexistenz ein Gegengewicht schaffen zu können: der Mensch, nicht nur allein Zweck und Ziel von Produktionsmethoden und deren mathematischen Gesetzmäßigkeiten, sondern selbstverwirklicht im Privaten, im Formenkanon assoziativen Denkens und Empfindens, in Übereinstimmung mit sich selbst, mit der Natur und der ihn umgebenden Gegenständlichkeit. Galt es doch, eine Alternative anzubieten, die auch einer "anderen Lebensart" Gelegenheit zur Selbstverwirklichung bot: Das "Ich", nicht determiniert vom Zwang mechanischer und funktioneller Zweckvorstellungen, sondern legitimiert aus den ureigensten Bedürfnissen wie Farbempfinden, Formensprache, Stilbewußtsein oder Gefühlsbetontheit.

Das Bewußtwerden der Seele, die Deutung des Traums, die Entwicklung der Psychoanalyse, die Entdeckungen der Graphologie sowie die ersten Ansätze der beginnenden Frauenemanzipation: In einer Zeit des Umbruchs hin zur Vermassung, Entfremdung und seriellen Fertigung waren dies die Säulen, auf denen sich das Programm für eine neue Religion, eine neue Moral, ein neues Kunstempfinden, ja einen neuen Kult formulieren ließ: Jugendstil - die Kunst des Seelenlebens - die Einheit von Leben und Kunst. Der Versuch, sämtliche Lebensbereiche des Menschen nicht nur neu zu formen und zu gestalten, sondern von innen, vom Zentrum her, zu durchdringen.

Die neuen Erkenntnisse der Psychoanalyse ließen sich in der Kunst des Jugendstils nicht leugnen. Immer mehr Artisten drängte es in die gläsernen Treib- und Gewächshäuser, um seltsam Pflanzliches, viel Wucherndes, ja vieldeutig Rankendes akribischen Studien zu unterziehen.

Glaubte man doch in den edlen und empfindsamen Gewächsen und Pflanzen, im Farn und im Blattwerk den Keim und den Herd all jener Auswüchse festmachen zu können, denen die damalige Gesellschaft mit immer mehr Unbehagen entgegensah: der Einflußsphäre der Psychologie. Wurde doch immer stärker deutlich, daß hinter den äußeren Erscheinungsformen und ihrer Symbolwelt eine rational nicht erfaßbare zweite Wirklichkeit lauerte, die mehr Einfluß auf sein Verhalten ausübte, als dies der Mensch bis dahin zu glauben gewohnt war. - Und so zog es in den letzten Sommernächten einer zuende gehenden Epoche die Künstler in die Glashäuser einer Innenwelt, um die wildwuchernden Triebe des menschlichen Seelenlebens ornamental zu formen, um die Wurzeln und die Blüten von Traum und Wirklichkeit visuell zu schönen, während das emanzipierte Weib das Tageslicht nicht scheute, um mit ganzem Einsatz und fast religiösem Eifer im Kunstgewerbe die Erlösung von der vorgestanzten Frauenrolle zu erfahren - ja, um im Jugendstilornament ein neues Glaubensbekenntnis zu suchen.

Das erklärt auch die enorme Verbreitung der überall entstandenen (und nicht selten bibliophilen) Kunstzeitschriften, die nicht nur wie Musterbücher des neuen Stils die Formvorstellungen des Zeitgefühls widerspiegelten, sondern geradezu als Katechismus der soeben ausgerufenen Religion gehandelt und interpretiert wurden.

Proklamiert wurde die Erlebniseinheit, das Gesamtkunstwerk, die Formung des gesamten Lebensstils. Manifest wurde die Sehnsucht nach der verlorenen Ursprünglichkeit, nach dem Stimmungsgehalt und dem Wunderbaren in der Märchen- und Sagenwelt. Gesucht wurde die vollkommene, die verzehrende Schönheit, die Harmonie und die Grazie der Bewegung, und letztlich eine von der Natur bestimmte, tragende Ordnung, die dem gesamten Leben und Empfinden des Menschen als Grundlage dienen sollte.

Die Kunst des Jugendstils stellte alles Pflanzliche zwar in den Mittelpunkt ihrer Ornamentik, ließ daneben jedoch abstrakte Formen zu, wenn auch meist nur solche mit vegetabilem Schwung oder Linienornamente, deren Bewegungsspiel auf langen, dünnen Stielen oder ihrer zügig geschwungenen Umrisse basierte. Die neu entdeckten Tiefen der Seele, die Überlagerungen unterschiedlicher Realitätsebenen, die freie Verbindung von Traumelementen, die diffuse Verwendung einer natürlichen Farbenpalette (entsprechend den Zwischentönen der im Traum erfahrenen Natur), sowie das Ausbrechen aus gewohnten formalen Dimensionen, ließen ein neues Sentiment, ein neues Ornament entstehen, eine Art Stempel, der trotz seiner Flächigkeit und Schattenlosigkeit und trotz seiner plakativen Wirkung einem Abdruck der Seele ähneln sollte.

Die Künstler des Jugendstils mußten geahnt haben, daß sie sich anschickten, das letzte Fest einer zu Tode geweihten Epoche auszustaffieren. Ein Fest, dessen Tanzfläche auf den Pfeilern rankender Blütenkelche wogte und schon deshalb nicht gegen Vergänglichkeit immun war, vielmehr umweht vom Hauch und vom Gesang eines frühen Todes. Folglich galt es, sinnlich und erotisch, manisch und leidenschaftlich einen elegischen Totentanz zu inszenieren, standen doch die Chargen des industriellen Neubeginns mit ihren Vollstreckungsbefehlen schon überall an den Saalausgängen bereit.

Die erhabenste und symbolyträchtigste Flora - die formale und wohl auch geistige Essenz des Jugendstils, die zweifellos ein nur sehr kurzes, aber üppiges Leben verheißen konnte - wurde kunst- und bedeutungsvoll drapiert, galt es doch ihre blasse und manierierte Schönheit ein letztes Mal erleben und bewundern zu dürfen. Das Hinsterben wollte man in vollen Zügen genießen: dem Tod keinen schlaffen, sondern einen reich ausstaffierten, einen wohlfeilen Körper darbieten.
    War nicht letztlich alles nur eine übernächtigte, fiebrige Illusion?
    Oder der über Nacht geborene Wille, der sich frühmorgens in den Tautropfen den Strahlen der Sonne entgegenzustellen versucht?

In diesem geistigen Klima und in diesem sozialen Umfeld ließ sich leicht viel Traditionelles überwinden, ließ sich Archaisches neben Klassisches, Fließendes neben Starres, Abendländisches neben Fernöstliches im Ornament einen. Das Ornament hatte hier nicht mehr nur zu schmücken, zu gliedern, zu betonen oder sich gar neutral zu verhalten. Hier durfte es sprießen, ranken, überwuchern, ausschlagen, eine eigene Gesetzmäßigkeit entwickeln, allesbeherrschender Mittelpunkt der Szene werden. Das Ornament nicht nur als Formelement, sondern als selbständige und souveräne Verkörperung des Inhalts selbst, mit einem spielerischen Hang zur Arroganz. In Anbetracht des nahen Endes spielten hierarchische Probleme wie Relation von Raum und Zeit, von Raum und Fläche oder von Form und Farbe nur noch eine untergeordnete Rolle. In dem Bemühen, durch den Jugendstil die festgefügte ästhetische Ordnung zu unterwandern und mit einem neuen Bewußtsein zu durchdringen, waren sie von nebensächlicher Bedeutung. Statt der "Form" stand jetzt die "Deformation" oder die Verwendung verschiedener Bild- und Realitätsebenen ohne Berücksichtigung der wirklichen Gegebenheiten im Vordergrund: das Ornament als Katalysator von Kunst und Psychologie, von Kunst und Leben, als Synthese von Wunsch und Wirklichkeit.

Das Wissen vom "Blühen und Vergehen", entsprechend dem vegetabilen Charakter des Jungendstils, erlaubte in der Kunst zuvor nie gekannte Freiheiten. Das stete Nahen der sich ausbreitenden neuen Industriegesellschaft drängte zur Eile. Und so begann dieser letzte Akt (letztlich schon ein Suchen nach der verlorenen Zeit), der das Abblühen einer kulturellen Episode schon einläutete. - Was war das Faszinierende, das Geheimnis und das Fluidum, das Erotische und das Narkotikum an der Epoche des Jugendstils? Ein Stil, der wie der Duft blühender Blumen in einer Tropennacht in wenigen Jahren seinen Elan, seine immense Phantasie und seinen unerschöpflichen Formenreichtum im Garten der Kunst des Occidents verschwendete. Ein Aufblühen - betörend wie der Duft der Orchidee, streng im Ornament der Lilie - ein neuer Stil: art nouveau / modern style / stile floreale.

Zwei Szenen aus der Literatur stellen sich ein: Der Mädchenreigen aus "Les filles du feu" von Gérard de Nerval und die letzte Ballnacht im Hause der Guermantes aus "A la recherche du temps perdu" von Marcel Proust. Sie bezeichnen einmal eine ferne Wurzel, sodann das Abblühen des Jugendstils. Die eine Szene zeichnet ein lebendes Ornament, ein Bild von Jugendlichkeit und Blütenduft. Sich öffnend wie Blütenkelche tanzen junge Mädchen im Rhythmus alt-überlieferter Chansons des Valois. Der Mädchenreigen bildet auf einer von hohen Bäumen umstandenen Rasenfläche ein sich laufend erneuerndes Muster. Die vom Mondlicht bestrahlten Tanzfiguren und die sie umgebende märchenhafte Szenerie lassen ein Ornament entstehen, das in der verfeinerten Grazie der Mädchengestalten gesteigert wird. Neben dieses Bild aus der Vorzeit ornamentaler Gestaltung, das Gérard de Nerval (Les filles du feu, Sylvie) entworfen hat, tritt - zeitlich schon zum Ausklang des Jugendstils - ein Gemälde von der Vergänglichkeit allen Blühens, erstarrt in einem kubischen Muster jähen Alters. Dem spontanen Erinnern von Marcel Proust (A la recherche du temps perdu; le temps retrouvé) an die Zeiten sensiblen Raffinements und nuancierter Andeutung stellen sich die Schatten der einstigen Zierde des Salons der Guermantes gegenüber, versammelt zu einer gespenstigen Maskerade, formiert zu trippelndem

Totentanz. Eine Szene fein drapierter Gerippe, vereint zur letzten Ballnacht vor dem Morgengrauen der aufbrechenden Industrialisierung. - Aufblühen und Verblühen verfestigen sich im Rhythmus eines Tanzes, wie ihn die Amerikanerin Loie Fuller in ihren "Serpentinentänzen" vorführte, zur abstrahierenden Form des Ornaments, das fließt, dann verharrt, dann um sich selber kreist, das ganze Leben durchwirkt. Überströmendes Wachsen, pflanzliche Asymmetrie, die Steigerung zu einer Ästhetisierung von Leben und Kunst, die sich sinnlich weiß und zu einer Ästhetik von Leben in der Vergänglichkeit stilisiert, einer Ausdrucksform, die mehr beansprucht, als ein neuer Stil der décadence zu sein. - Der Jugendstil öffnet sich mit einem unbändigen Formwillen dem Ornament. Er findet in der sensitiv-schwingenden Linie jenen Reiz von Abstraktheit und runenhaftem Ursprung, die die "art nouveau" sogleich als neues, eigenständiges Ausdrucksmittel wählt. Der Jugendstil bedient sich der vegetabilen Formsprache und erzeugt in der Verbindung von exotischer Pflanze, wie dem Frauenschuh und der Iris, mit Symbolen des Weiblichen eine erotische Spannung, die graphisch raumübergreifend wirkt, die Gegenstände kostbar und transparent werden läßt, Vasen und Gläser mit floralen Ornamenten überzieht, und sie sprechen läßt, wie die "verres parlants" von Emile Gallé.

Der treffend genannnte "Stile Floreale" bringt Schmuckstücke von bezaubernder Zartheit hervor, er hängt Lampen von blühender Schwerelosigkeit über die Zugänge zur Pariser Métro. Ein bleibendes Signum der "art nouveau". Eine andere europäische Variante des Jugendstils folgt der rhythmischen Linie der Natur, wiegt fließende Formen wie Algengewächse in einem unsichtbaren, submarinen Reich, entledigt die Objekte ihrer Dinghaftigkeit. Das organische Ornament rankt sich zum magischen Zeichen.

Das Ornament dient nicht der äußeren Dekoration, es ist Strukturelement, verwandelt die Alltagswelt in immer freiere Rhythmen. Das Ornament wird zum Funktionsträger: es formt den Türgriff zur Gebärde, es empfängt den Gast auf der ersten Treppenstufe des Hauses mit einladender Geste und führt ihn kaum spürbar weiter in Innenräume mit hohen, lichten Glaskuppeln, wo großzügig gespannte Stoffe und Tapeten mit delikaten Mustern ein neues Lebensgefühl suggerieren. - Die pflanzliche Herkunft der Ornamente, überzeichnet in zerbrechlicher Zartheit, läßt einen Hauch floralen Wachsens spüren. Sie wecken sensuelle Empfindungen, streifen den Tastsinn, evozieren Düfte, verbreiten opakes Licht. Der verfeinerten Steigerung der Formen entspricht eine sich ständig nuancierende Farbgebung, die abgestimmt und blaß die Zwischentöne transluziden Leuchtens sucht. - Die Ästhetisierung des Lebens winkt weiter in eine Welt der Ästhetik der Vergänglichkeit, in eine sanftsüchtige Traumwelt, wo sich die Grenzen von Traum und Wirklichkeit im reinen Ornament auflösen, das - hier abstrakt, dort einen Blütenkelch zeichnend, aus dem sich anmutigende Mädchen- oder Knabenkörper emporranken - zum Traum im Traum hinleiten will.

Die neuen, bio-"logischen" Formen weisen auf eine vorrationale, vegetabile Existenz hin. Eine Ahnung von Vergänglichkeit haftet ihren Gestalten an. Gestalten, die sich in einem fremdartig irisierenden Licht gefallen und in die Utopie eines Kunst-Lebens münden, das hinreißend schön und vergänglich den zauberhaften Duft exotischer Pflanzen verströmt.

Durante el ocaso del siglo pasado, poco antes de la definitiva afirmación de la máquina y la técnica, y en vísperas de la revolución industrial con su inexorable imposición de la mecanización y racionalización, con el alud de productos de masa en el mercado y, como consecuencia, una aplastante despersonalización de las formas, expresiones y creatividad individuales; en Europa, el arte - sobre todo la artesanía y el arte decorativo - intentaron, durante un breve lapso, oponerse a aquel monstruo desgarrador.

Ante la imposibilidad de detener el desarrollo técnico y material, se pretendió explotar las posibilidades del conflicto para así alcanzar, mediante el arte, una simbiosis que pudiera armonizar, en forma unísona, el mundo de la "técnica--función-racionalidad", con el del "hombre-alma-naturaleza". Basándose en la coexistencia, se abrigaba la esperanza de obtener una compensación: por un lado el hombre, no sólo como meta y fin de métodos productivos y su correspondiente matemática legalidad; y por el otro la realización, en el ámbito privado, bajo forma de pensamiento asociativo y sensaciones en concierto consigo, con la naturaleza y la cultura circundante.

Se trataba de ofrecer, justamente, una válida alternativa que incluyera la posibilidad de realizar "otro modo de vida". El "yo", no determinado por la obligación de ideas mecánicas y funcionales, sino legítimamente autorizado a considerar las necesidades primordiales como el sentido del color, el lenguaje de las formas, la conciencia del estilo y el juego de las emociones. El conocimiento del inconsciente, la interpretación de los sueños, el desarrollo del psicoanálisis, el descubrimiento de la grafología, como así el vislumbrarse de la incipiente emancipación de la mujer, en una era convertida a la masificación, a la alienación y a la producción en serie; eran las columnas sobre las que fue posible construir una nueva religión, una nueva moral, una sensibilidad artística nueva e, inclusive, un nuevo culto: El estilo floreal - arte de la vida espiritual - cohesión de arte y vida. El anhelo de recrear la totalidad de la experiencia humana, no sólo diversamente sino, por sobre todo, penetrando en ella partiendo desde su centro. Las entonces nuevas experiencias del psicoanálisis no fueron rechazadas, lógicamente, por el Art Nouveau. Una cantidad de artistas, en permanente aumento, se volcaban al detallado estudio de la flora exótica de los jardines botánicos, centrando la atencíon en la exuberancia de las trepadoras. Existía la convicción de poder identificar en el noble y sensible follaje, el centro y origen de todo lo que la sociedad contemporánea miraba con creciente disgusto, es decir, la esfera de la influencia ejercida por la psicología.

Era cada vez más evidente que, escondida entre las aparentes formas exteriores y su simbólico mundo, se mantenía en guardia una irrealidad irracional que influía sobre el comportamiento del hombre, con mayor intensidad e importancia de la que el mismo pudiera creer. Por lo tanto, en las noches estivas de un época que veía las últimas luces de su ocaso, los artistas transformaban en ornamento la vida psíquica del hombre, beatificando las flores de los sueños y la realidad. Mientras tanto la mujer emancipada no temía las claridades del nuevo amanecer para así conocer, con real compromiso y un fervor casi religioso, la resolución de su papel protagónico prescrito, en otras palabras; en la ornamentación del Art Nouveau, buscaba un nuevo sendero de Fe. Este hecho explica la enorme difusión de revistas de arte que surgieron en ese período distinguiéndose, además, por su alta calidad. No se trataba de simples catálogos que reflejaran las formulaciones creativas del gusto y tendencias de entonces sino que, y así se las trataba, debían ser interpretadas como el verdadero catecismo de un religión recién proclamada.

Tal proclamación era la unidad de las experiencias, el trabajo total del arte, la formulación de un completo estilo de vida. Fue así manifestado el deseo de una espontaneidad perdida entre las impresiones de las maravillas en un mundo de fábulas y leyendas. Se estaba en la búsqueda de una total y sólida belleza, de la armonía y gracia del movimiento y, como norte principal, de un determinado orden armónico con la naturaleza, que pudiera surgir como puente fundamental entre la totalidad de la vida y la sensibilidad del ser humano.

En la médula de su teoría, el Art Nouveau situaba el mundo vegetal, otorgando también espacio a las formas abstractas que, fundamentalmente, tuvieran largos y sutiles movimientos con contornos ondulantes.

Las entonces recién descubiertas profundidades de la psiquis: Diferentes planos de una realidad sobrepuesta; la libre asociación de elementos oníricos; el uso de una paleta casi toda filtrada por colores naturales (correspondientes a los tonos intermedios de la naturaleza, como vividos durante el sueño) y la evasión de formales dimensiones habituales. Todo ello determinó el nacimiento de una nueva sensación, una nueva manera de adornar; una especie de emblema que, a pesar de su monótona superficie - falta de sombras y un efecto casi de cartel - debía recrear la impresión de la psiquis.

Los artistas del Art Nouveau eran concientes de estar preparando el escenario para el último acto de una era que llegaba a su fin. Se representaría una fiesta cuyo salón de baile apoyaba sobre cimientos de cálices y capullos de plantas trepadoras.

Justamente efímeras, las movía el anhelo de una muerte prematura: era necesario preparar el escenario con decorados sensuales, eróticos, con manías y pasiones para actuar una elegante Danza Fúnebre. Los dirigentes de la era industrial - con una orden ejecutiva en mano - estaban listos para salir a bailar.

La flora más sublime e impregnada de símbolos - la formal y espiritual esencia del Art Nouveau que, sin lugar a dudas podía prometer una vida breve; la más breve y abundante de todas - era artística y significativamente preparada para ser admirada por última vez.

Lo que se deseaba era acercarse a la muerte con un atuendo formal; no llegar a la muerte con un cuerpo rengo, sino con uno bien dotado y lozano. ¿No era todo esto, quizás, una cansada y febril ilusión? ¿O bien era un deseo, madurado de noche, que al amanecer trataba de convertirse en gotas de rocío, para oponerse a los rayos del sol? En este clima espiritual, como así en tal ambiente social, era fácil superar lo tradicional, era fácil unificar, con decoraciones, lo clásico con lo arcaico; lo fluctuante con lo rigido; Occidente con el lejano Oriente. La decoración no debía limitarse sólamente a su función ornamental, ya sea acentuando o quedando neutral. Podía florecer, crecer, trepar, reproducirse, desarrollarse con sus propias leyes, y converstirse en el punto dominante de la escena. Ornamento no sólo como elemento formal sino como personalización independiente y soberana del contenido mismo, con una disposición casi juguetona hacia la arrogancia.

En consideración del inevitable final, los problemas de jerarquía, entre las relaciones tiempo-lugar, espacio-superficie, como así forma-color, tenían un rol secundario. En la intensión de usar el Art Nouveau para infiltrar el orden estético establecido de infundir una nueva conciencia, aquellos problemas adquirían un significado accidental. En lugar de forma se hablaba de "deformación", o bien la representación de figuras sin considerar las proporciones reales: la ornamentación considerada como catalizadora del arte y de la psicología; del arte y de la vida como síntesis de deseo y realidad.

El concimiento del "florecer y desvanecer", de acuerdo a la condición botánica del Art Nouveau, permitió libertades en el arte, desconocidas hasta entonces. La constante expansión de la nueva sociedad industrial aceleró el paso. Así comenzó ste último acto - al concluir la búsqueda del tiempo perdido - anunciando el final de un episodio cultural.

¿Cuál era el encanto, el secreto, lo fluido, lo narcótico y lo erótico en la época del Art Nouveau? Un estilo que, en pocos años, a la par del perfume de las flores que nacen en una noche tropical, ha desperdiciado su brío, su inmensa fantasía y su inagotable riqueza de formas en el jardín del arte occidental. Un florilegio - seductor como el perfume de la orquídea, severo como la simple ornamentación del lirio - un nuevo estilo: Art Nouveau, Jugendstil, stile liberty.

Dos escenas literarias acuden al recuerdo: la danza de las doncellas en "Les filles du feu", de Gérard de Nerval, y el último baile en la casa de los Guermantes, de la obra "A la recherche du temps perdu", de Marcel Proust. La primera es el amanecer del Art Nouveau; la segunda es el ocaso.

Las doncellas representan una escena de ornamento vital; imagen de juventud floridamente perfumada. Las doncellas bailan al ritmo de tradicionales canciones. Sobre un prado verde, enmarcado por altos arbustos, la ronda de las doncellas forma un modelo continuamente renovable. Las figuras danzantes, iluminadas por un claro de luna en un escenario de fábulas, crean ornamentos dibujados con la gracia de los refinados cuerpos de las jóvenes doncellas.

Juntamente a la representación de Gérard de Nerval, de los primeros tiempos de la creatividad ornamental (Les filles du feu, Sylvie) podemos colocar otra que, en cambio, pertenece al período final del Art Nouveau: un retrato de florescente fugacidad, casi entumecido en un modelo cúbico arcaico. Recordando espontáneamente a Marcel Proust (A la recherche du temps perdu, le temps retrouvé); a aquel tiempo de refinada sensibilidad y tímidos indicios, se oponen, ahora, las sombras de los ornamentos de antaño en los salones de los Guermantes, en derredor a una mesa en cuadro espectral, como en formación previa a comenzar una briosa danza de muerte. Una escena de esqueletos, delicadamente disfrazados, reunidos en la última noche de baile, antes del gris amanecer de la era industrial.

Por lo tanto el florecer y desflorecer se componen en un ritmo de danza, como lo representó la coreógrafa norteamericana Loie Fuller en sus "bailes serpiginosos", cuya forma abstracta es la primera ornamentación que se desliza, para luego persistir y girar sobre sí misma, penetrando la vida entera. Crecimiento desbordante, asimetría del mundo vegetal, enaltecimiento de vida y arte conciente de su sensibilidad, estilizado de la vida efímera; una nueva forma de expresión que pretende ser mucho más que un nuevo estilo decadente.

El Art Nouveau se manifiesta con una incontenible voluptuosidad en sus formas ornamentales. En la sensual y flexuosa línea encuentra el encanto de lo abstracto y lo original, que inmediatamente adopta como propio medio expresivo. Este estilo habla el idioma de las formas vegetales y, en combinación con plantas exóticas como Escarpines de la Virgen y Lirios, genera una tensión erótica que gráficamente produce el efecto de una difusión en el espacio, que favorece la creación de objetos preciosos y transparentes; vasos, jarrones y demás cristalería adornada con ornamentos fugaces, de esta manera les da la palabra, como los "verres parlants" de Emile Gallé.

El llamado estilo floreal crea verdaderas joyas de encantadora ternura. En los ingresos de la metropolitana de París, cuelga lámparas de etérea y floreciente fluidez: emblema duradero del Art Nouveau.

Otra variante europea del estilo floreal sigue el juego rítmico de la naturaleza, entreteje formas fluctuantes como las algas marinas en un invisible reino submarino; priva a los objetos de su real materialismo. Las ornamentaciones orgánicas se convierten en un signo mágico. La ornamentación no es en función de la decoración externa, sino que es estructural y transforma la vida cotidiana en ritmos más libres; ornamentación que se convierte en sujeto de función: cambia una manija en un gesto, recibe al huésped frente a las escaleras y con un indicio de bienvenida lo conduce, imperceptiblemente, en un espacio interno dotado de cúpulas altas y vidrios luminosos, donde tejidos y tapices con delicados motivos sugieren un nuevo sentido de vida.

El origen vegetal de las ornamentaciones distinguidas por una suerte de frágil ternura, emana un respiro de crecimiento floreal; solicitan la percepción sensorial sus ornamentos, mezclan el sentido del tacto, evocan fragancias y difunden una opaca luminosidad. Al refinado desarrollo de las formas se acompaña una coloración delicadamente sombreada la cual, pálida y esfumada, exije los tonos intermedios de la iluminación transparente.

La estetización de la vida alude a un mundo efímero, a un mundo nostálgico de sueños en el cual las fronteras - entre sueño y realidad - se disuelven en ornamentación pura que, aquí abstracto, allá muestra el cáliz de una flor que brota del encantador cuerpo de una joven o un doncella, conducidos de un sueño a otro. Las nuevas bio-"lógicas" formas indican una existencia vegetal prerracional que se agrega a ellas. Formas éstas que se destacan en una luminosa iridación desconocida, desembocando en la utopía de una vida artística donde la mágica fragancia de plantas exóticas, en su belleza extenuante y efímera, se desparrama con lumínico sentido.

C'était au tournant du siècle, encore un peu avant l'affirmation définitive de la machine et de la technique, à la veille de la révolution industrielle avec son inéluctable contrainte à la mécanisation et à la rationalisation, ses produits fabriqués en série et son inexorable nivellement de toutes les formes d'expression verbale et figurative; alors qu'en Europe l'art (surtout l'artisanat artistique et les arts appliqués) tentait pendant une brève période de s'opposer à ce moloch omnivore qu'était le nouvel esprit des temps. Mais le progrès technico-matériel étant irrépressible, on s'efforça tout au moins de tirer parti du conflit pour réaliser, à travers l'art, une symbiose susceptible de concilier les deux univers, "technique-fonctionnel-rationnel" et "individuel-psychique-naturel". Grâce à leur coexistence, on espérait pouvoir créer un contrepoids: l'individu, non seulement comme objet et but des processus productifs et de leur légitimité mathématique, mais se réalisant dans le domaine privé selon des normes formelles de pensée et de sensibilité associatives, en harmonie avec lui-même, avec la nature et avec le caractère concret de son environnement. Il s'agissait, au fond, d'offrir une alternative permettant aussi à un "autre mode de vie" de se réaliser: le "moi" non pas déterminé par la contrainte de concepts utilitaristes, mécaniques et fonctionnels, mais légitimé, au contraire, par ses propres exigences fondamentales, telles que sa sensibilité chromatique, le language des formes, son sens du style et son émotivité.

Conscientisation psychique, interprétation des rêves, évolution de la psychanalyse, découverte de la graphologie et premiers rudiments de l'émancipation féminine naissante: à une époque où les bouleversements entraînaient le nivellement général, l'aliénation et les productions en grande série, c'étaient là les colonnes sur lesquelles s'édifiait le programme d'une religion nouvelle, d'une nouvelle morale, d'un nouveau sens artistique, voire même d'un nouveau culte: l'art nouveau - art de la vie psychique - union de la vie et de l'art. Une démarche tendant non seulement à reformer et à restructurer toutes les sphères de la vie humaine, mais encore à les pénétrer par le dedans, par le centre.

L'influence des récentes découvertes de la psychanalyse sur l'art nouveau était indéniable. Un nombre toujours croissant d'artistes éprouvait le besoin d'aller dans les serres et forceries en verre pour y soumettre des plantes rares, une végétation luxuriante, et même d'ambiguës tiges grimpantes à des études méticuleuses. Car on croyait pouvoir découvrir dans les plantes et végétaux nobles et sensibles, dans les fougères et les feuillages, le germe et le foyer de toute une débauche d'excès que la société d'alors voyait venir avec une angoisse toujours croissante: les excès de l'influence exercée par la psychologie. Cependant, il devenait de plus en plus évident que derrière les manifestations extérieures et leur univers symbolique, une seconde réalité était à l'affût, rationnellement insaisissable, qui exerçait sur le comportement de l'individu une influence bien plus grande que celle à laquelle il croyait être habitué. Et voilà que dans les dernières nuits d'été d'une époque à son déclin, les artistes éprouvaient la nostalgie des serres chaudes d'un univers intérieur, où ils pourraient donner une forme ornementale aux instincts sauvages dont pullule la vie psychique et embellir visuellement les racines et les floraisons du rêve et de la réalité; tandis que la femme émancipée ne craignait pas de s'exposer à la lumière du jour pour expérimenter, en s'engageant à fond, et avec un zèle quasi religieux, dans la pratique de l'art décoratif, la rédemption du rôle féminin pré-matricé - et même pour chercher dans l'ornement selon l'art nouveau, une nouvelle profession de foi. Ceci explique également la diffusion des périodiques d'art (même parmi les bibliographes) qui paraissent un peu partout, et qui non seulement reflètent les concepts de forme du sentiment contemporain, à l'instar des catalogues du nouveau style, mais sont considérés et interprétés comme de véritables catéchismes de la religion qui vient d'être proclamée.

Ce qu'on proclamait, c'était l'unité de l'expérience, l'oeuvre artistique totale, le façonnement du style de vie dans son ensemble. Ce qui était manifeste, c'était la nostalgie de la spontanéité perdue, des états d'âme et du merveilleux contenus dans le monde féerique et mythique. Ce qu'on recherchait, c'était la beauté parfaite et dévorante, l'harmonie et la grâce du mouvement, et en fin de compte un ordre déterminé par la nature, pouvant servir de base à l'ensemble de la vie et des sentiments de l'individu.

S'il est vrai que l'art nouveau a mis au centre de sa création ornementale tout ce qui est végétation, il a fait place également aux formes abstraites, même s'il se limitait, en général, à celles qui présentaient une envolée végétale, ou des ornements linéaires dont le jeu des mouvements naissait à partir de tiges longues et minces, ou de leurs contours hardiment élancés. Les profondeurs de l'âme, récemment découvertes, les superpositions de différents plans de la réalité, la libre association d'éléments oniriques, l'ample usage d'un chromatisme naturel (correspondant aux tons intermédiaires de la nature vécue en rêve), et l'évasion hors des dimensions formelles habituelles, ont donné naissance à un sentiment nouveau, à un nouveau type d'ornement, à une sorte de cachet qui, malgré son absence de relief et d'ombres, malgré l'effet aplatissant qu'il produit devait ressembler à une empreinte de l'âme.

Les artistes de l'art nouveau ont sans doute pressenti qu'ils se préparaient à organiser la dernière fête d'une époque vouée à la mort. Une fête dont la piste de danse ondoyait sur des piliers faits de calices de fleurs grimpantes, et qui, pour cette raison même, n'était donc pas immunisée contre l'éphémère, mais était caressée par le souffle et par le chant d'une mort prochaine. Il s'agissait par conséquent d'orchestrer sensuellement et érotiquement, de façon obsessionnelle et passionnée, une danse macabre élégiaque, même si toutes les issues de la salle étaient gardées par les laquais de la nouvelle ère industrielle, munis de leurs mandats d'exécution.

La flore la plus sublime, et symboliquement la plus prégnante - l'essence formelle et même spirituelle de l'art nouveau, qui ne pouvait certes promettre qu'une vie brève, mais opulente - était drapée avec art, dans une pose lourde de sens, mais c'était uniquement pour faire vivre et admirer une dernière fois sa beauté blafarde et maniérée. On tenait à savourer à pleins traits son trépas: présenter à la mort un corps non pas avachi, mais richement et élégamment paré.

Tout celà n'était-il, après tout, qu'une pure illusion nocturne et fébrile? Ou était-ce au contraire le dessein, formé pendant la nuit, de s'exposer, le matin venu, aux rayons du soleil dans les gouttes de rosée? Dans ce climat spirituel et dans cet environnement social, on pouvait aisément vaincre bien des traditions, et unir dans l'ornement l'archaïque au classi-

que, le fluide o figé, l'occidental à l'extrême-oriental. Ici, l'ornement ne se bornait plus à la simple décoration, à la structuration,
à l'emphase, ou encore à conserver une attitude neutre. Il pouvait
à loisir croître, grimper, envahir, bourgeonner, développer sa propre légitimité,
occuper le centre prédominant de la scène. L'ornement non pas comme élément
de la forme seulement, mais comme personnification autonome et souveraine
du contenu lui-même, avec un penchant ludique à l'arrogance.

En raison de la fin prochaine, les problèmes de hiérarchie, tels que les rapports
espace-temps, espace-superficie, ou forme-couleur, ne jouent plus qu'un rôle
subordonné. Dans le contexte des efforts tendant à permettre à l'art nouveau de
s'infiltrer dans les structures cohérentes de l'ordre esthétique établi, et à pénétrer
celui-ci d'une conscience nouvelle, ces problèmes avaient une importance secon-
daire. Au lieu de la "forme" il y avait la "déformation", ou l'utilisation de divers
plans de l'image et de la réalité, sans trop d'égards pour les faits concrets qui
occupaient la vedette: l'ornement catalyseur de l'art et de la psychologie, de l'art
et de la vie, synthèse du désir et de la réalité.

Savoir ce que sont "la floraison et le flétrissement", selon le caractère végétal de
l'art nouveau, permettait de prendre des libertés inconnues jusqu'alors dans le
domaine de l'art. L'approche de la nouvelle société industrielle en expansion, que
rien n'arrêtait, incitait à se hâter. Et ainsi le rideau s'est levé sur ce dernier acte
(qui, d'ailleurs, était déjà une quête du temps perdu), carillonnant dès à présent
l'agonie d'un épisode culturel.

Qu'avait donc de fascinant, de mystérieux et de fluide, d'érotique et de narcoti-
que, l'époque de l'art nouveau? Un art semblable au parfum de certaines fleurs é-
panouies par une nuit d'été tropical, qui, en quelques années, a gaspillé son élan,
son immense fantaisie et l'inépuisable richesse de ses formes dans l'art occidental. Une floraison - capiteuse comme le parfum de l'orchidée, sévère comme l'ornement du lis -un style nouveau: Jugendstil - modern style - stile floreale.

Deux scènes empruntées à la littérature nous viennent à l'esprit: la ronde des jeunes filles, dans "Les filles du feu", de Gérard de Nerval, et le dernier bal de nuit
chez les Guermantes, dans "A la recherche du temps perdu" de Marcel Proust.
Elles évoquent d'abord une racine lointaine de l'art nouveau, et ensuite son dépé-
rissement. La première scène est l'esquisse d'un ornement vivant, une image de
jeunesse et de parfum floral . S'épanouissant comme des calices de fleurs, les
jeunes filles dansent au rythme d'anciennes chansons du Valois. La ronde évolue
sur un tapis herbeux entouré d'arbres de haut fût, en dessinant un motif inces-
samment renouvelé. Les danseuses, baignées par la lumière lunaire, et le décor
féérique qui les entoure créent un ensemble ornemental que rehausse la grâce
des figures féminines. A côté de ce tableau de la préhistoire de l'art ornemental,
conçu par Gérard de Nerval (Les filles du feu, Sylvie), prend place - chronologi-
quement au moment où l'art nouveau est déjà à son terme - une peinture repro-
duisant le caractère éphèmere de toute floraison, figée dans un modèle cubique
qui porte en son sein le germe de sa caducité. La mémoire involontaire de Proust
(A la recherche du temps perdu; Le temps retrouvé), rappelant une époque de
raffinements délicats et d'allusions nuancées, fait pendant aux
ombres des décorations d'autrefois qui ornent le salon des Guermantes, rassemblées en une mascarade fantômatique, dessinant

une danse macabre qui évolue en trottinant. Une scène peuplée de squelettes élégamment drapés, réunis pour un dernier bal de nuit, avant l'aube de l'ère industrielle naissante. Epanouissement et étiolement se concrétisent en un rythme de danse semblable à celle qu'exécute Loïe Fuller dans ses "Danses en lacets" en une forme abstractive de l'ornement, qui s'écoule, se fige, tourne autour d'elle-même, s'enchevêtrant dans tout le tissu de la vie. C'est une croissance débordante, une asymétrie végétale, une intensification qui aboutit à l'esthétisation de la vie et de l'art, qui devient sensuelle et se stylise en une esthétique de vie dans l'éphémère, en une forme d'expression qui veut être autre chose qu'un nouveau style de la décadence. L'art nouveau s'ouvre à l'ornement avec la volonté inflexible de lui donner des formes nouvelles. Il découvre dans la ligne sensitive-ondulante l'attrait de l'abstraction et de l'origine runique et il l'a aussitôt adoptée comme moyen autonome d'expression. Ce style se sert du language des formes végétales, et en unissant des plantes exotiques, comme le sabot de Vénus ou l'iris, à des symboles féminins, il crée une tension érotique qui envahit graphiquement l'espace, donne de la valeur et de la transparence aux objets, habille d'ornements floraux les vases et les verres, et leur confère le don de la parole, à l'instar des "verres parlants" d'Emile Gallé.

Le "style floral", au nom on ne peut mieux choisi, met en valeur des bijoux d'une délicatesse ravissante, et suspend des lampes d'une splendide apesanteur audessus des entrées du métro parisien, signe durable de l'art nouveau.

Dans une autre variante européenne, il épouse la ligne rythmique de la nature, berce des formes mouvantes semblables à des algues dans un royaume sous-marin invisible, vide les choses de leur matérialité. L'ornement organique se hausse au niveau du signe magique. Il ne sert pas à la décoration externe; c'est un élément structurel qui transforme l'univers habituel en rythmes de plus en plus libres. Il devient une forme matérielle de la fonction lorsqu'il moule la poignée de porte sur le geste, accueille affablement les invités au bas de l'escalier et les conduit discrètement à l'intérieur, sous les coupoles de verre hautes et claires, où des étoffes et des tapisseries aux dessins délicats, généreusement déployées, évoquent une nouvelle joie de vivre. Grâce à leur origine végétale, les ornements se surpassent en finesse fragile et nous font deviner la présence d'un souffle émanant d'une poussée florale. Ils éveillent en nous des sensations sensuelles, effleurent la sensibilité tactile, évoquent des parfums, diffusent une lumière opaque. Le nuancement incessant de la coloration, qui cherche dans la variété des assortiments et dans la pâleur des tons les demi-teintes d'une luminosité translucide, correspond à l'intensification raffinée et graduelle des formes.

L'esthétisation de la vie se manifeste encore dans un univers de l'esthétique de l'éphèmere, dans un monde onirique plein de douceur enivrante, où les limites entre le rêve et la réalité se dissolvent dans l'ornement pur qui veut nous conduire - ici sous une forme abstraite, là en esquissant un calice de fleur d'où émergent des corps charmants de jeunes filles et d'enfants - vers un rêve à l'intérieur du rêve. Les nouvelles formes bio-"logiques" nous parlent d'une existence prérationnelle et végétale. Le pressentiment de l'éphémère imprègne leurs figures. Des figures qui se complaisent dans une étrange lumière irisante, et aboutissent dans l'utopie d'une vie artificielle dont la beauté ravissante et éphémère répand un parfum magique de plantes exotiques.

XXX

XXXI

The plates
in this volume derive from
original undated portfolio editions
created by unknown artists
between the years
1900 - 1910.

*

These editions were:

"Neue farbige Vorlagen
für die Textilindustrie"
and
"Moderne Blumen-Ornamentik"
edited by
Christian Stoll, Germany
and
"Neue Anregungen für
textilen Flächenschmuck"
edited by
Schulz & Co., Germany

*

The cover
of this volume was
created and developed
in the Studio & Laboratory
of Edition Belvedere in Rome, Italy.

The commentary to this volume
was composed
by

Wolfgang H. Hageney
and
Gundolf Fahl

*

1984

145

146

147

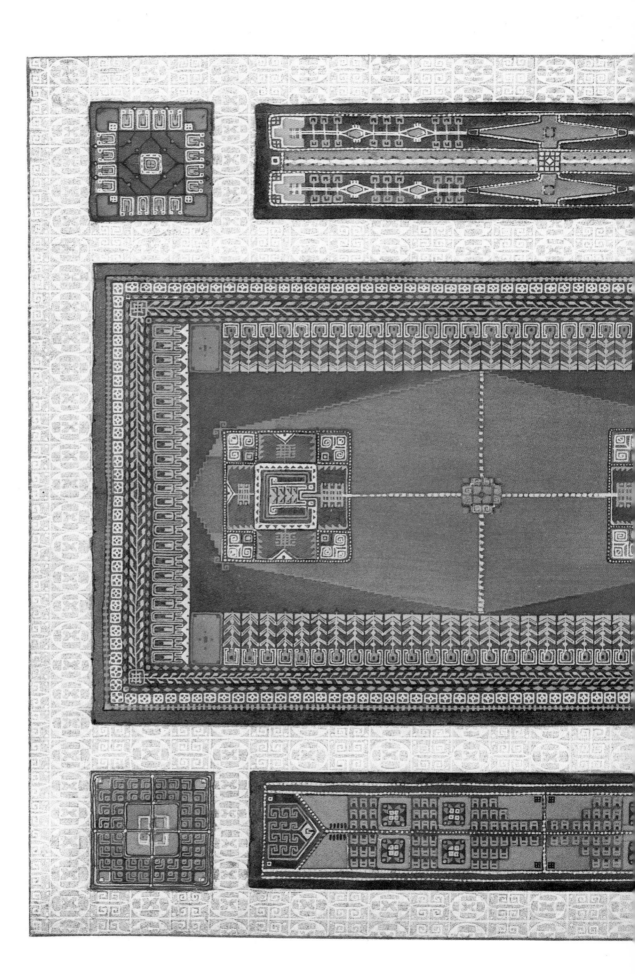

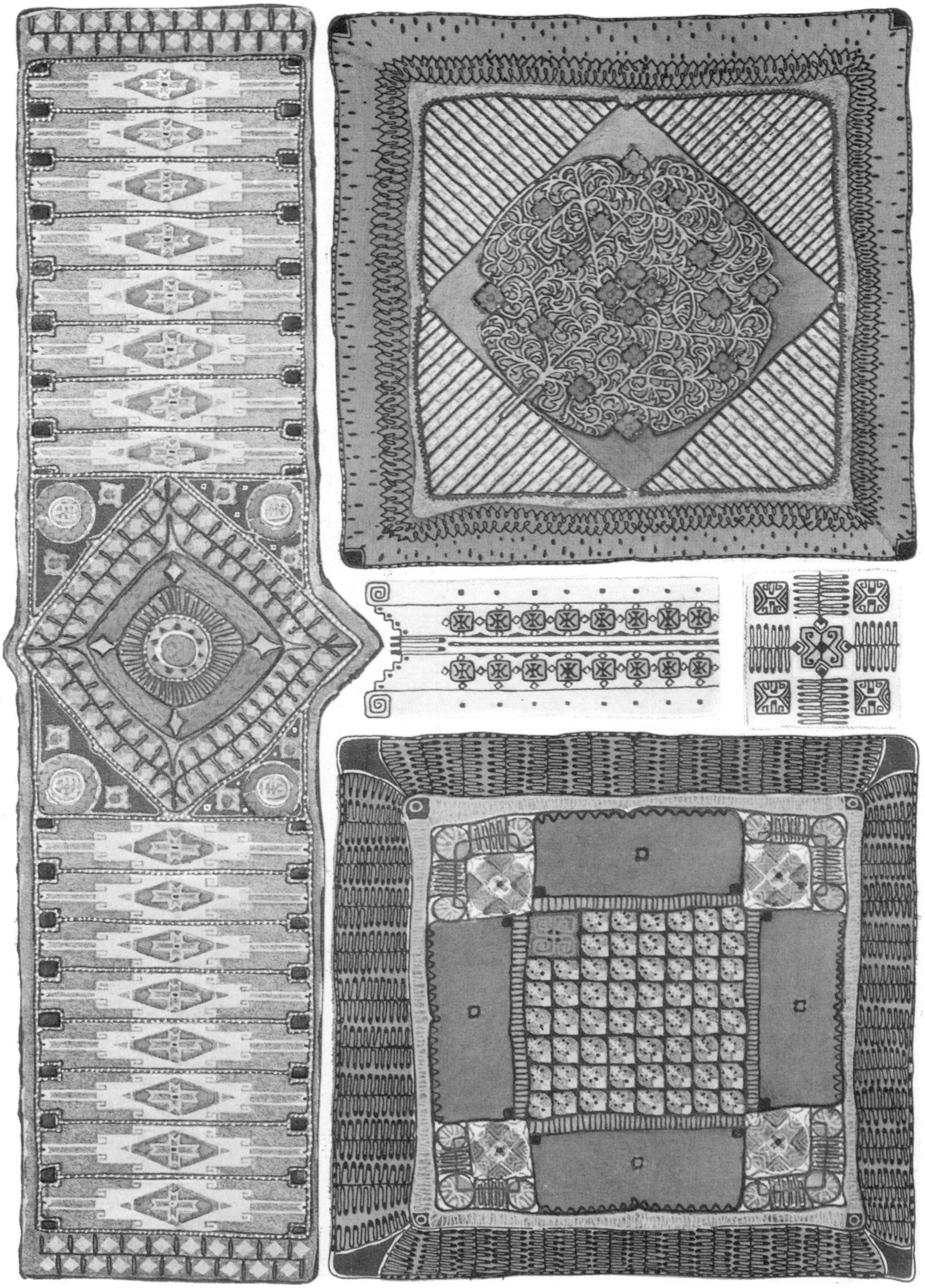

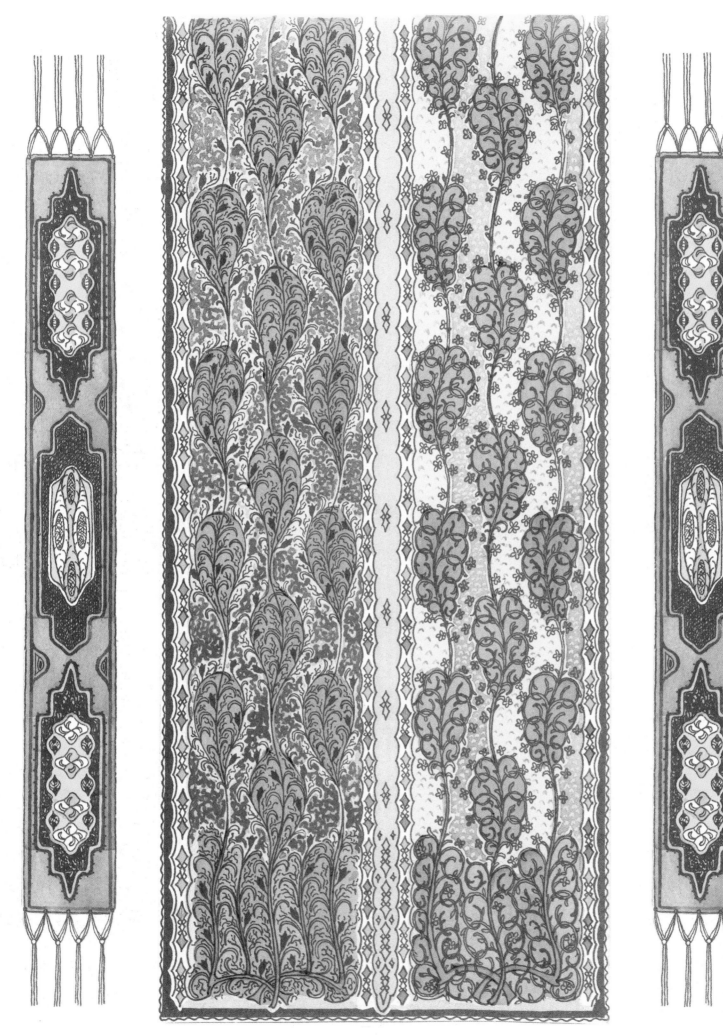

152

153

154

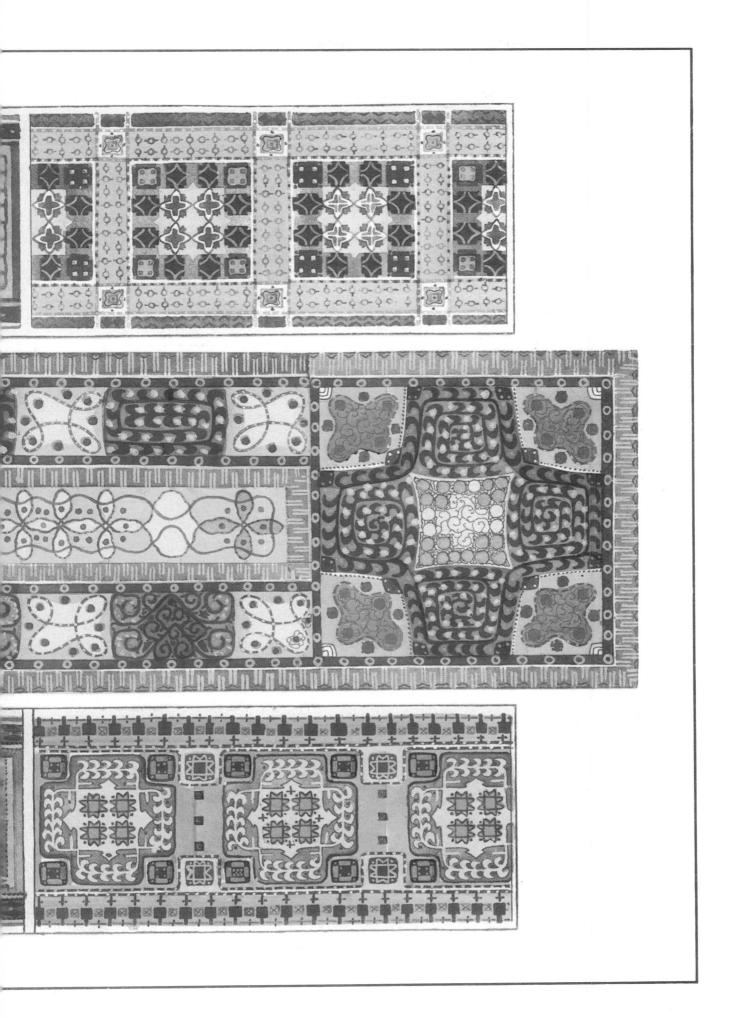

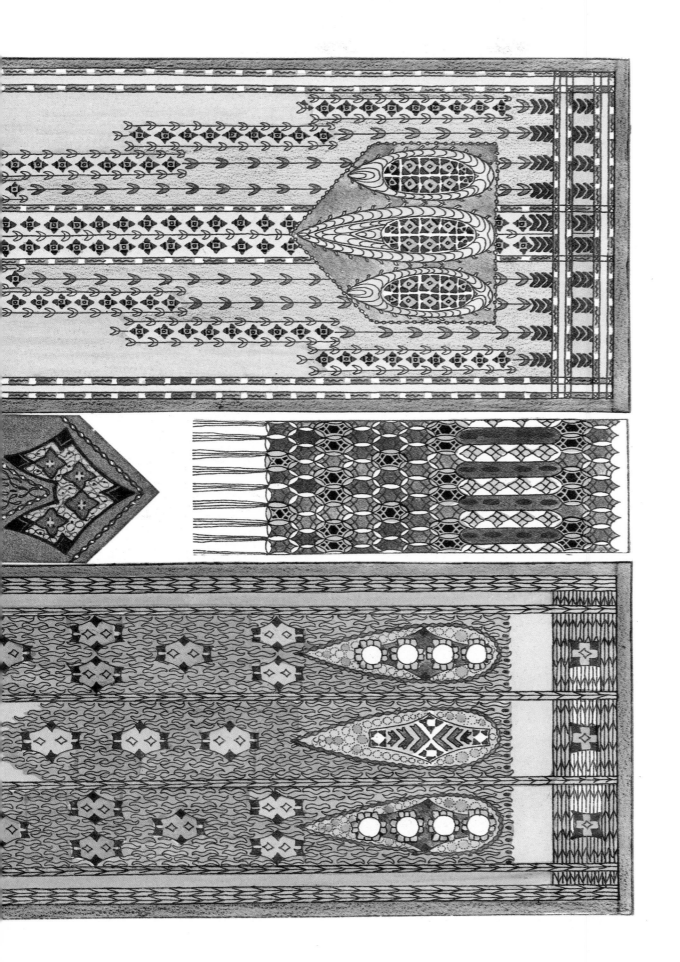

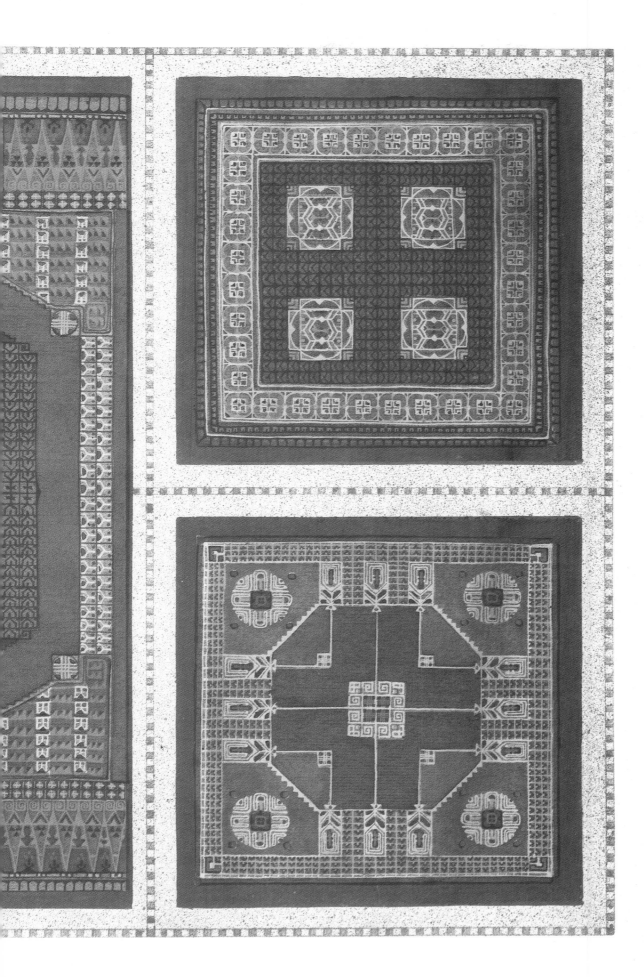

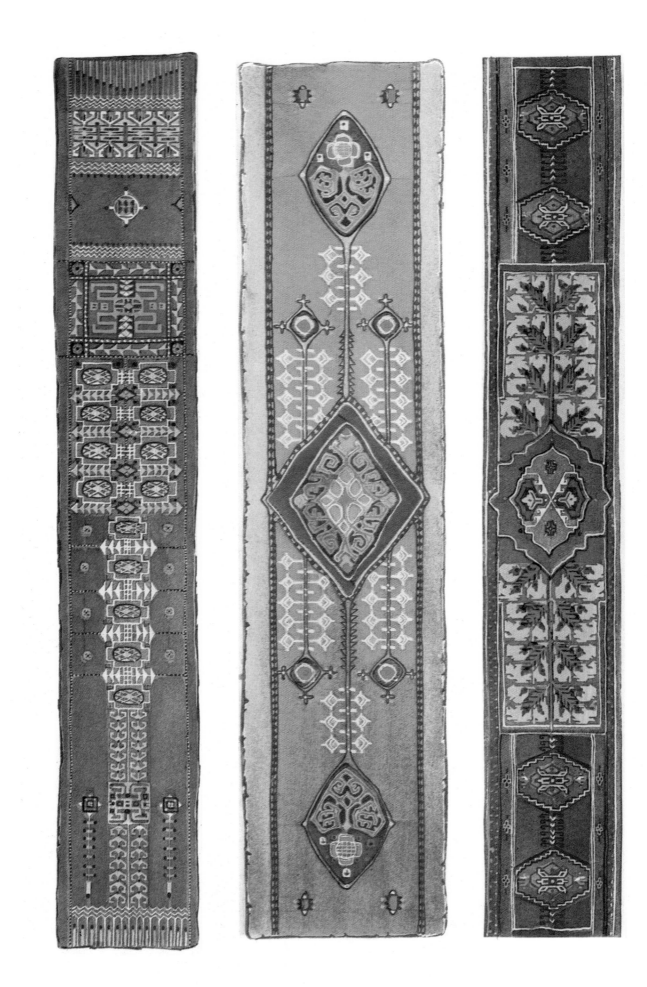

160

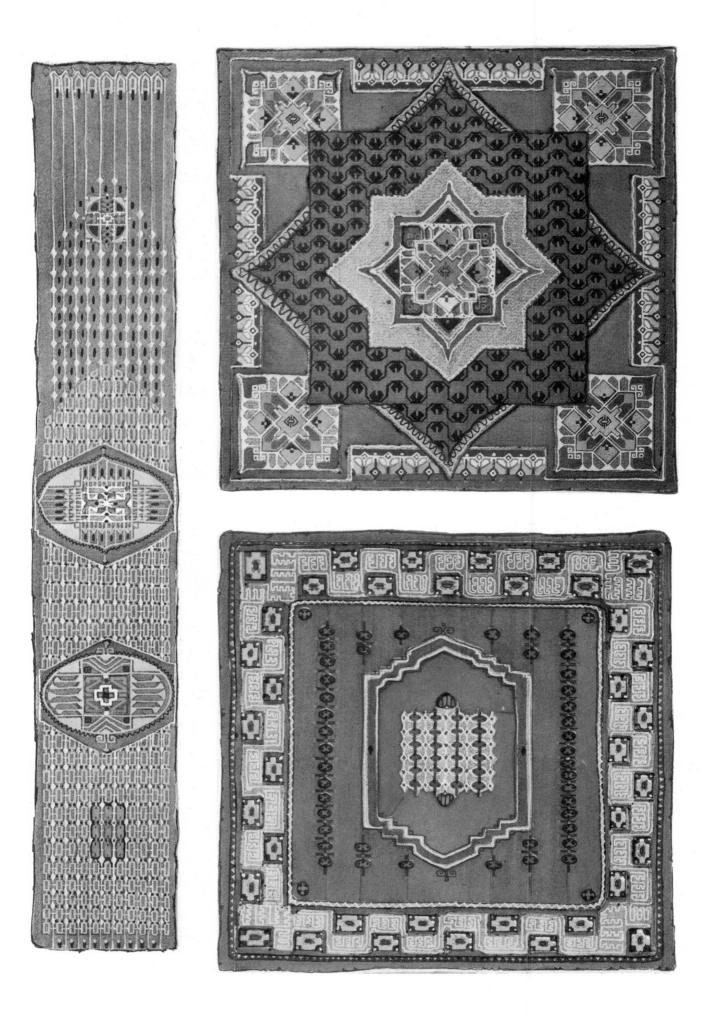

162

164

166

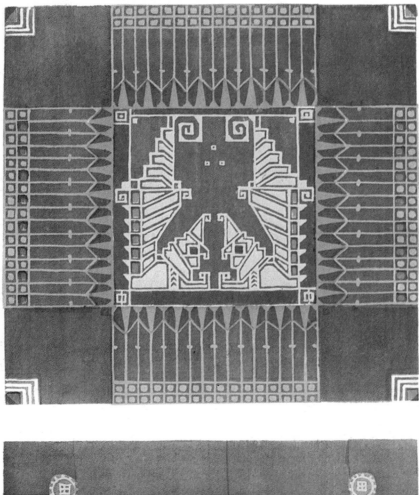

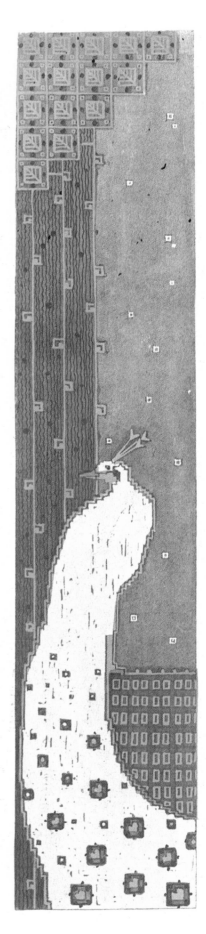

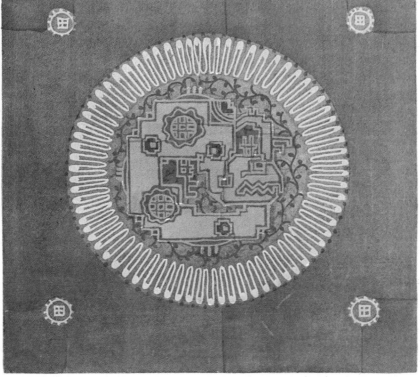

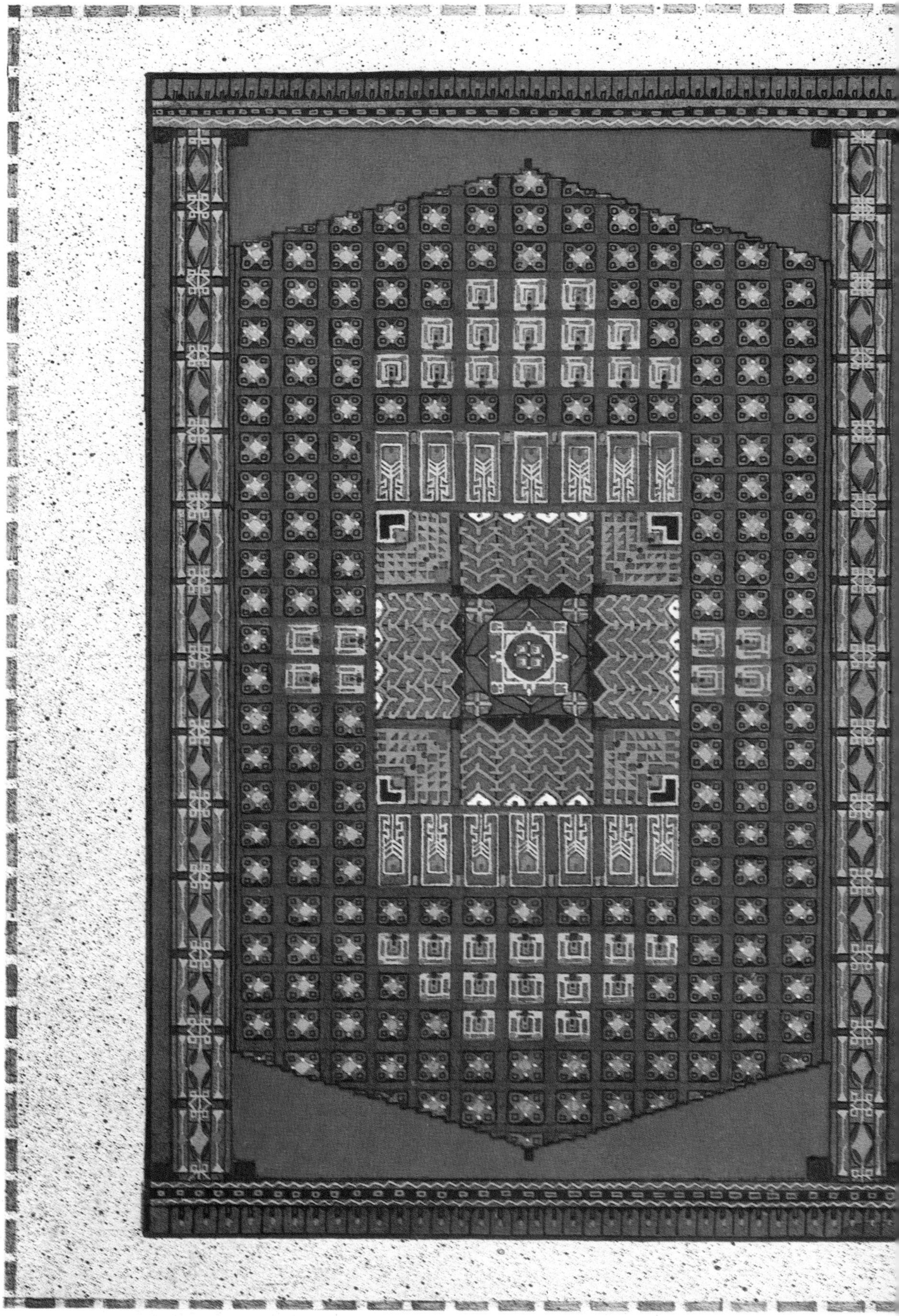

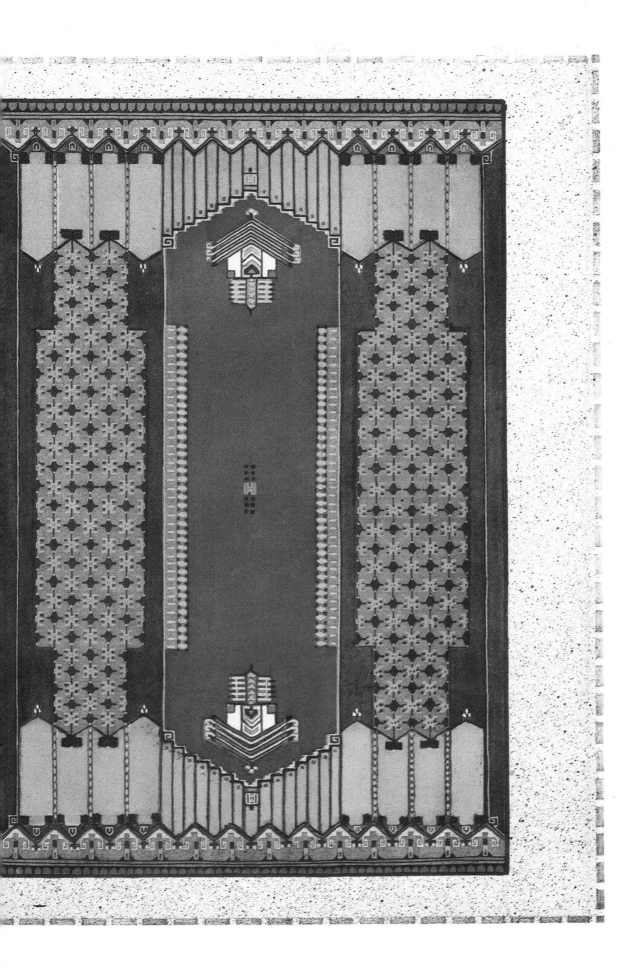

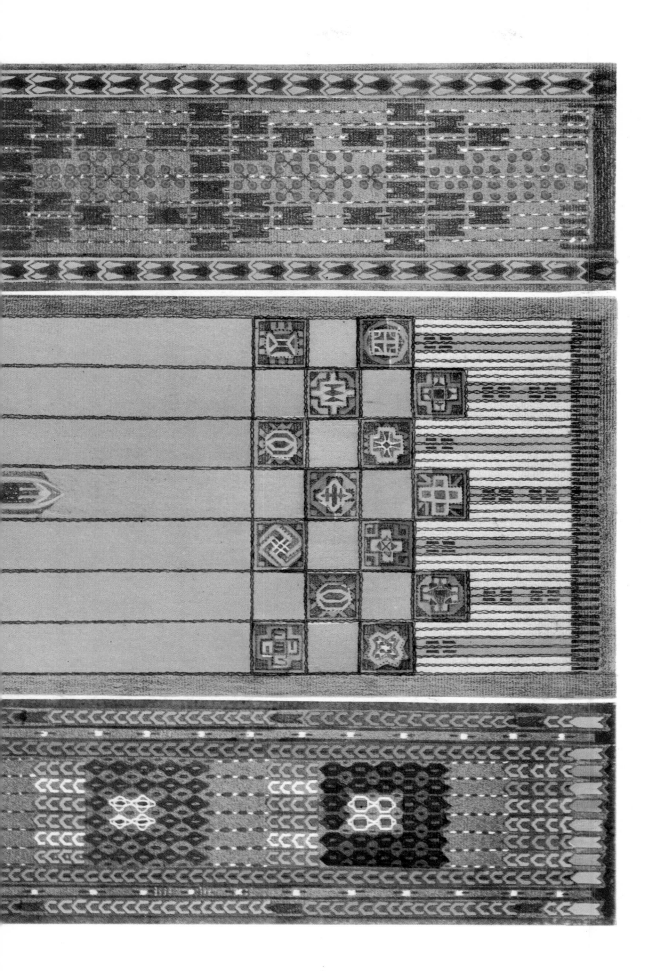

175

176

178

179

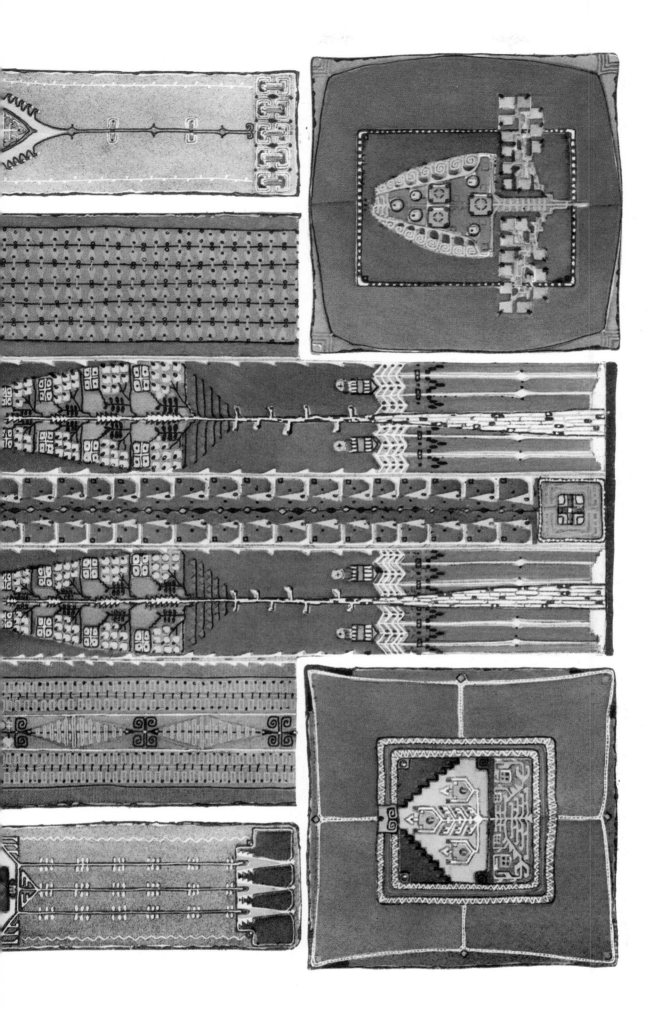

181

182

183

184

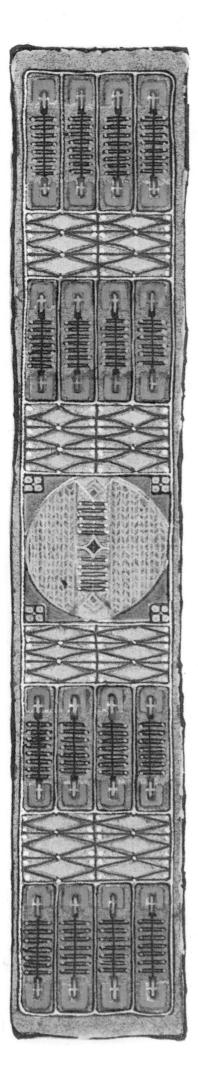

185

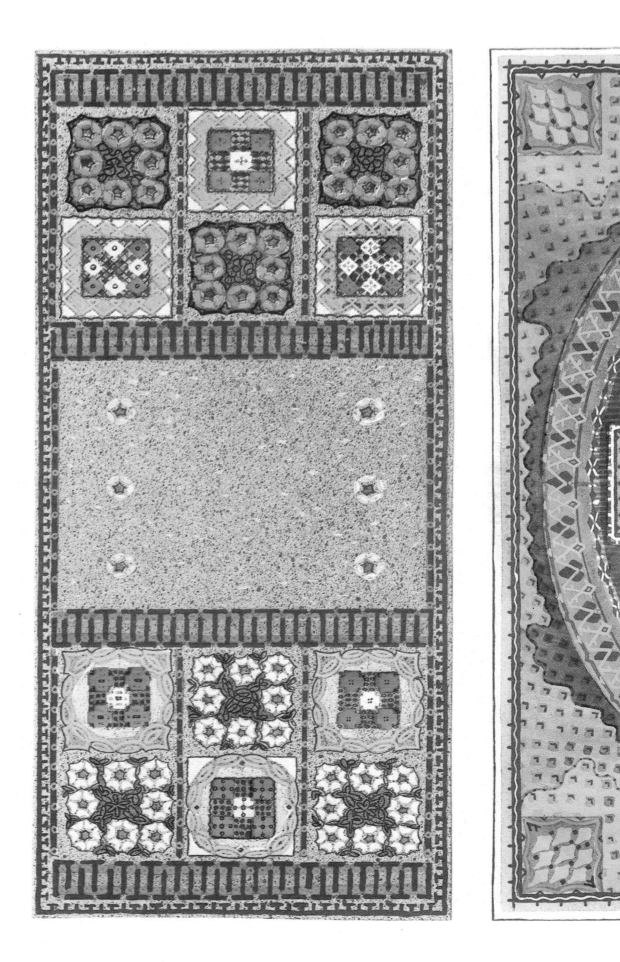

186

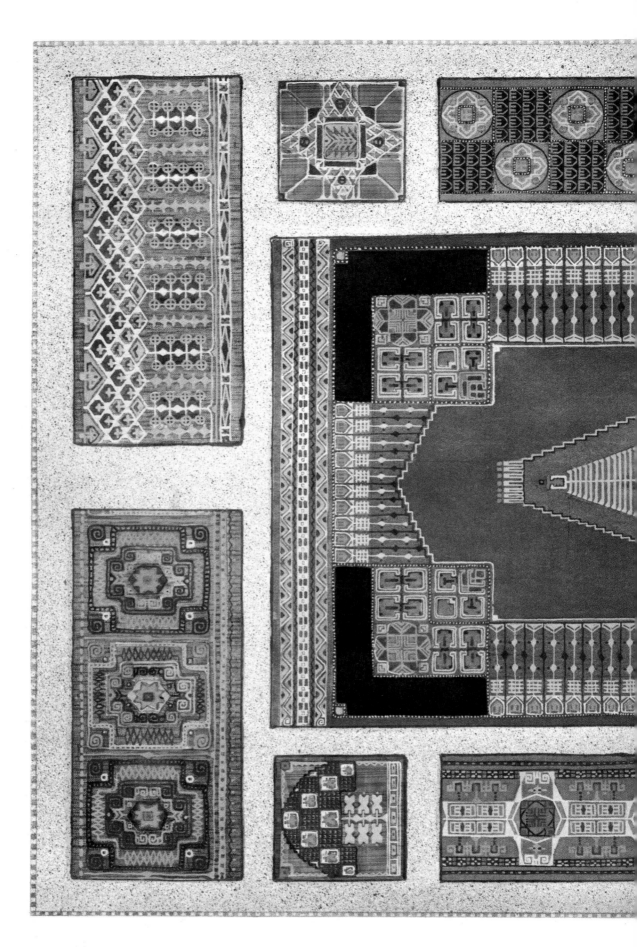

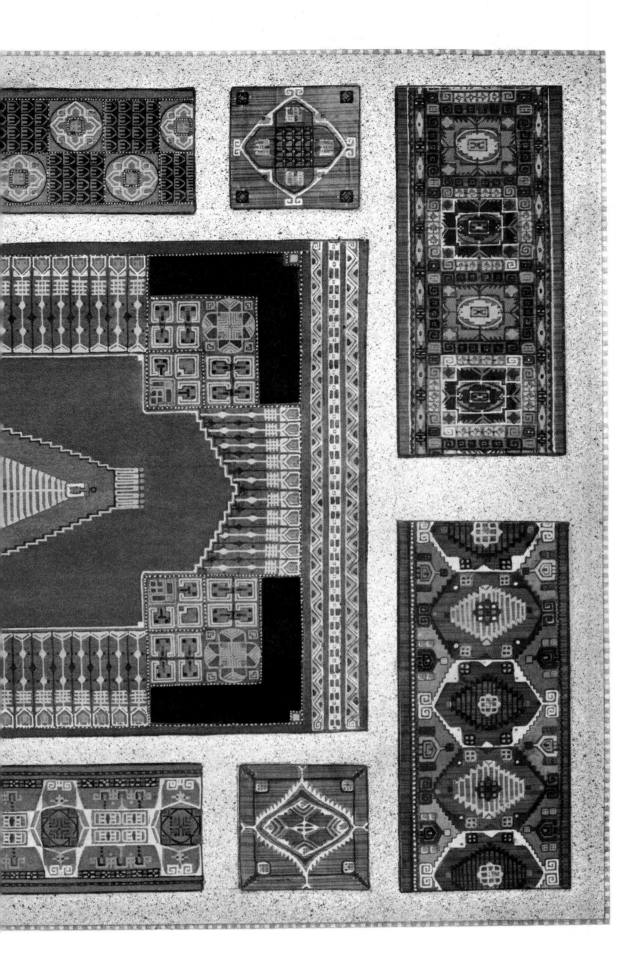

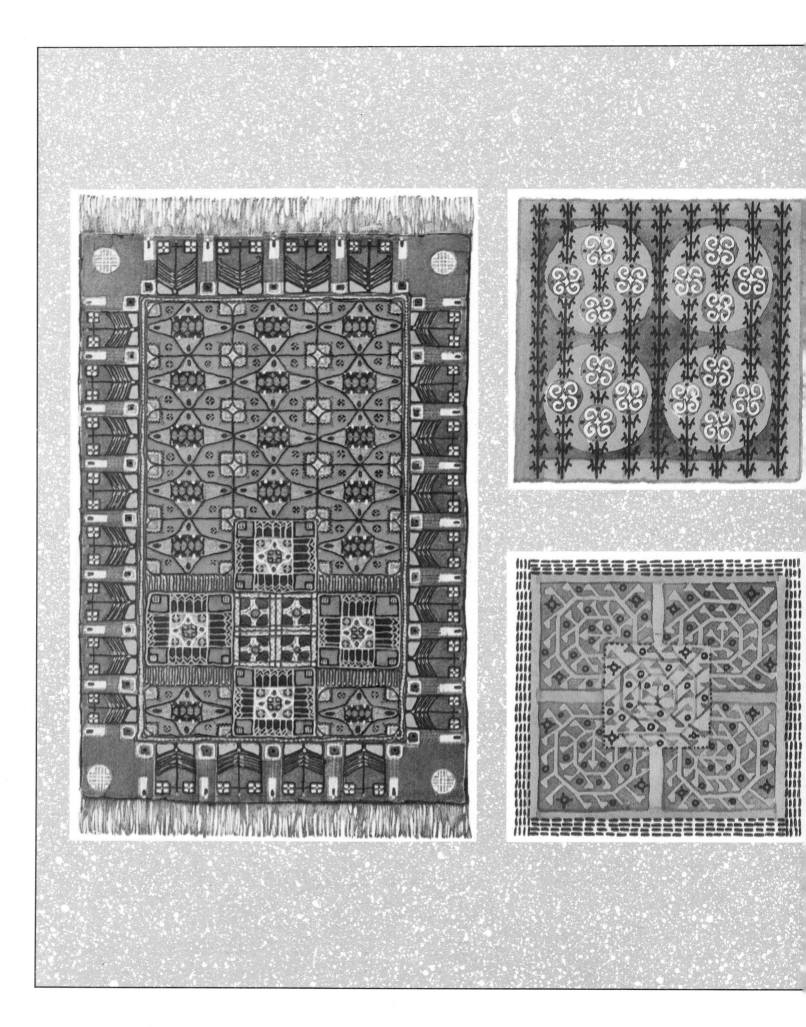

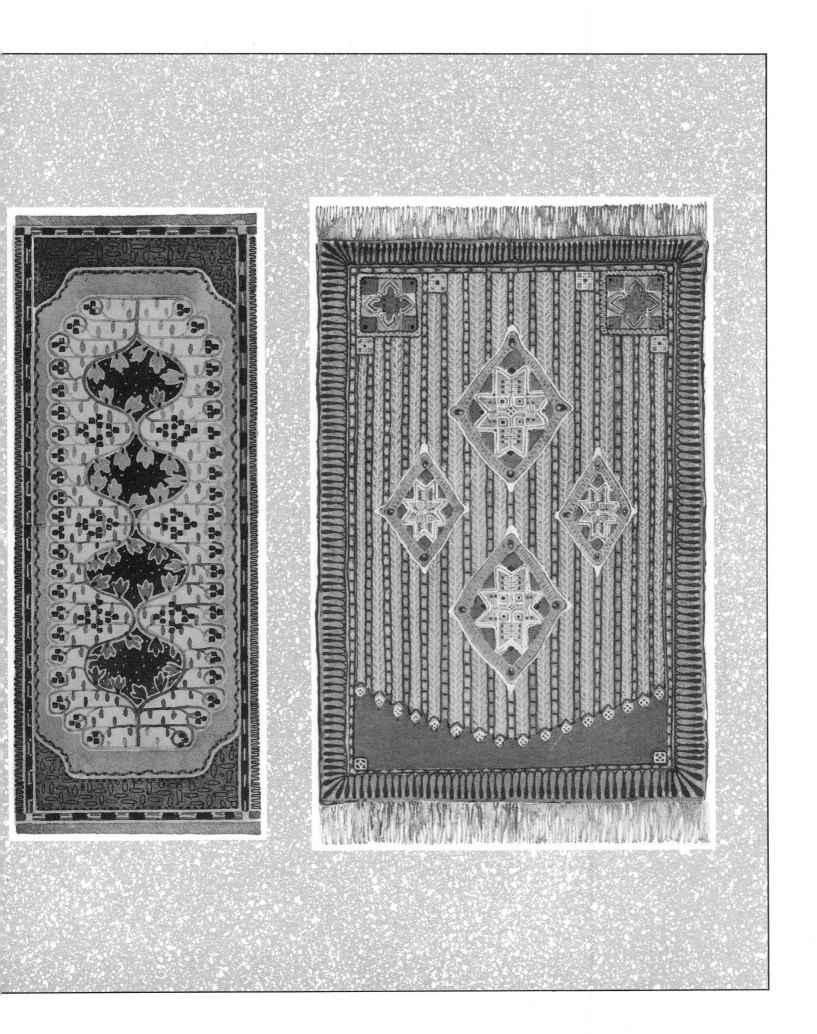

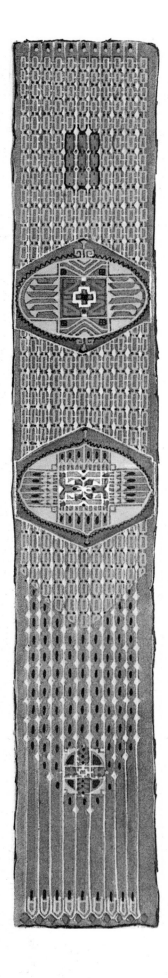
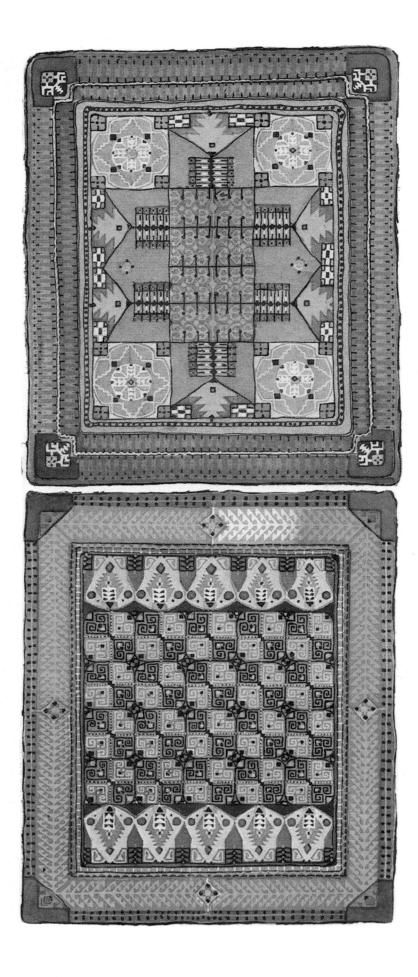

192

193

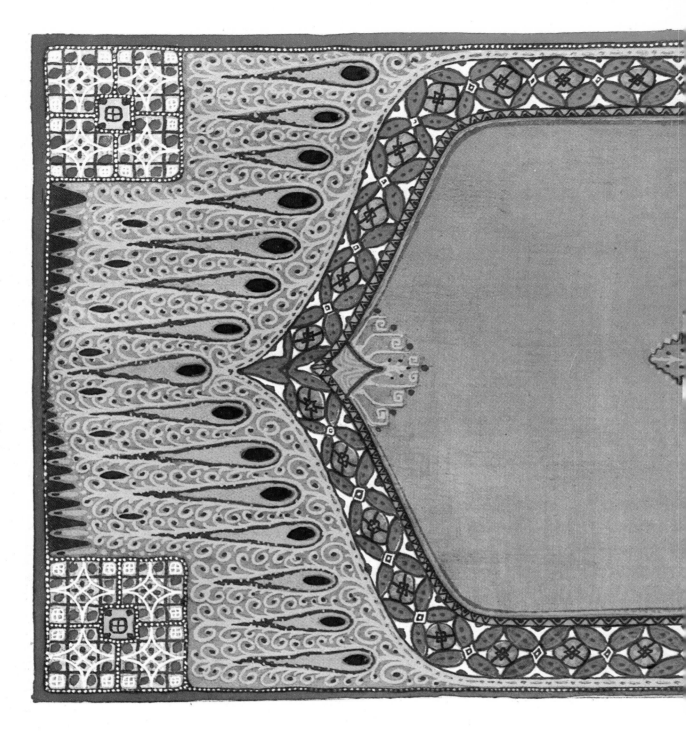

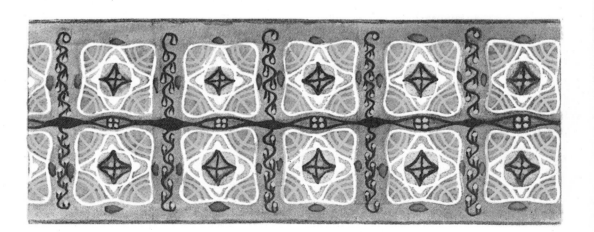

194

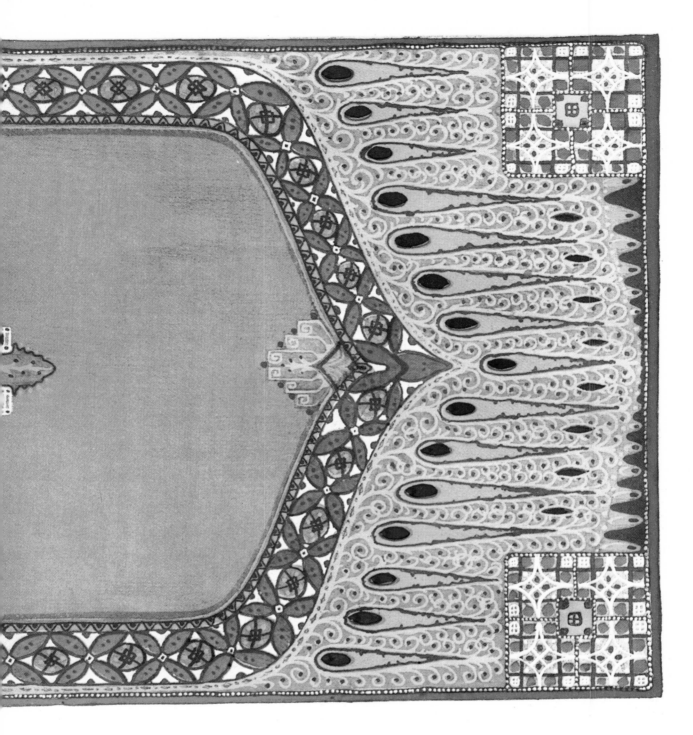

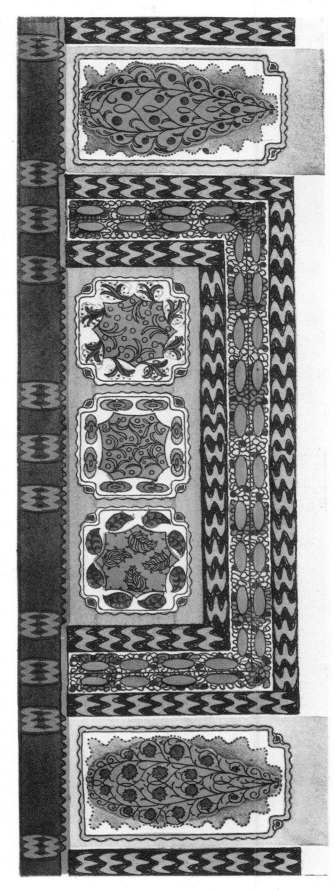

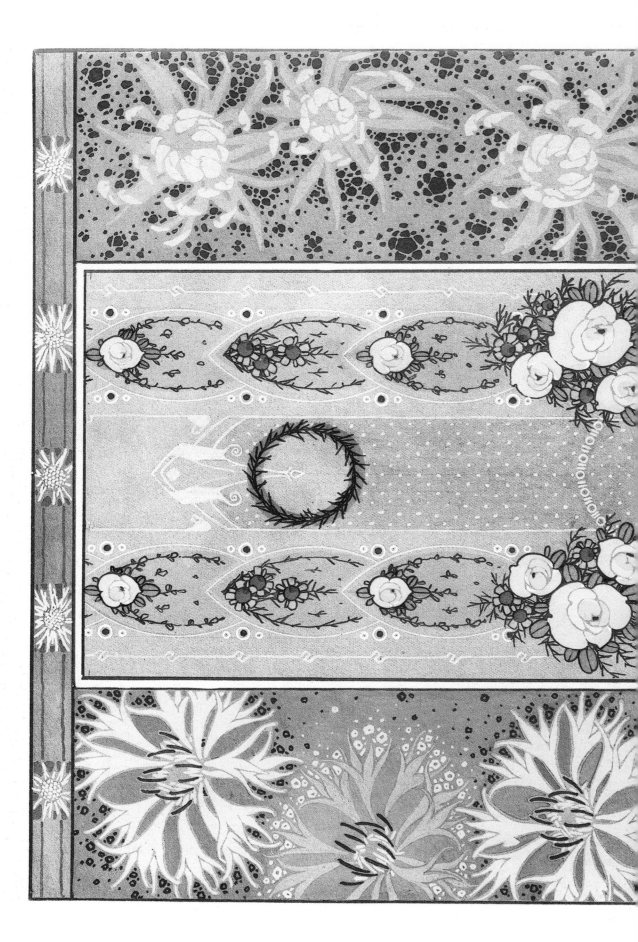

199

200

EDITION BELVEDERE

DESIGN BOOKS

MADE IN ITALY

...SIMPLY THE BEST...

Design
Club

FASHION TEXTILES GRAPHIC DESIGN
PHOTOGRAPHY LAYOUT DECORATION
ADVERTISING STYLING ILLUSTRATION
ORNAMENTS INTERIOR ARCHITECTURE

Good Design Books are hard to find. It takes you time and money to get the right images & references you need for your work. But now you can have it all more easily. Choose simply the best in its field: Belvedere-Design-Books, "made in Italy". Go, and ask for the DESIGN CLUB, and you will get a special offer (free of charge) immediately. It will surprise you.

E' difficile trovare buoni design books. Ci vuole tempo e denaro per avere le immagini e le idee giuste. Ma adesso è tutto più facile. Scegliete solamente il meglio: i Belvedere-Design-Books, "made in Italy". Chiedete del DESIGN-CLUB e avrete subito & gratis delle offerte eccezionali che vi sorprenderanno.

Gute Designbücher sind schwierig zu finden. Es erfordert oft viel Zeit und Geld, um an die richtigen Ideen & Vorlagen zu gelangen. Doch jetzt ist alles viel leichter. Wählen Sie einfach das Beste: Belvedere-Design-Books, "made in Italy". Erkundigen Sie sich nach dem DESIGN-CLUB und Sie werden unverzüglich & kostenlos ein Spezial-Angebot erhalten, das Sie überraschen wird.

BELVEDERE

DECOR

GRAPHIC FLOWER VOL. 1

...GNS
TH SIC
& STRIPES
ARIATIONS
TEXTILE & DECORATION
BELVEDERE

BELVEDERE

BELVEDERE

AFRICA VOL. 1

PHOTO-FASHION

BELVEDERE

GRAPHICOLOR
300 GRAPHICAL MOTIFS WITH FANTASY ALL IN COLOR VOL 2

...STUMES
FEMALE 1037 - 1870

BELVEDERE

BELVEDERE

Bouquets

BELVEDERE

FRESCO VOL. 2

BELVEDERE

ARCHI "TEXTURE"

BELVEDERE

BELVEDERE

books for fashion, decoration & graphic design...

BELVEDERE

DESIGNER'S NOTEBOOK

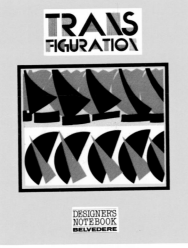

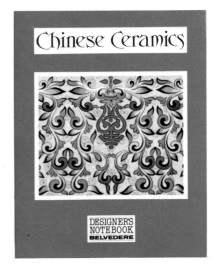

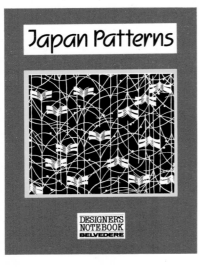

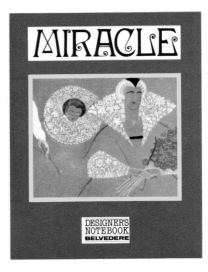

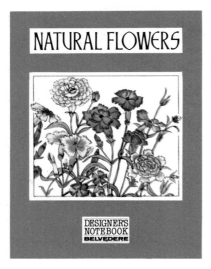

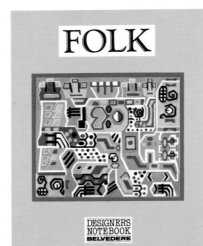

BELVEDERE